THE WAY OF FENG SHUI

THE WAY OF FENG SHUI

Harmony, Health, Wealth and Happiness

Philippa Waring

Souvenir Press

First published 1993 by Souvenir Press Ltd.,
43 Great Russell Street, London WC1B 3PA
and simultaneously in Canada

Reprinted 1994
Reprinted 1995
Reprinted 1996

ISBN 0 285 63124 1

Photoset by Rowland Phototypesetting Ltd.,
Bury St Edmunds, Suffolk
Printed in Great Britain by
The Guernsey Press Co. Ltd., Guernsey, Channel Islands

Feng Shui symbol for Happiness

'The most important factors in life are Fate, Luck, Feng Shui, Virtue and Education.

Old Chinese Proverb

'Feng Shui is the art of locating tombs, cities and houses auspiciously. Mountains, hills, water courses, groves and neighbouring buildings can be useful either in channelling the male Yang influences or in deflecting them.'

Funk and Wagnalls Dictionary

CONTENTS

ACKNOWLEDGEMENTS

The writing of this book has only been made possible by the careful instruction and generosity of a number of Chinese experts in Feng Shui, including Wong Siew Hong, Jiang Ping Jie, Wang Chao Chuan and Kwok Man Ho. Among Western writers who have also aided my study have been John Michell, Stephen Skinner, Sue Ellicott, Chris Partridge, Jonathan Sale, Nicholas Roe and Jocasta Shakespeare. I am grateful to Chicago University Press for permission to quote from the Raymond Van Over edition of the *I Ching*, and to Thames & Hudson Ltd for the extract from *The Ancient Science of Geomancy* by Nigel Pennick. My special thanks are also due to my publishers, whose help during the writing of this book was of great assistance in enabling me to make this ancient and complex Chinese art accessible to contemporary Western readers.

P. W.

風 水
PREFACE

This book could change your life. The aims of Feng Shui, 'the Art of Living in Harmony', are to enable men and women to find their ideal living environment and through this attain health, prosperity and happiness. It is an art—a 'Science' to some of its keenest exponents—that has been in existence for almost three thousand years, drawn from some of the most basic elements of life. Today, thanks to its sound psychological and environmental principles, it is finding a whole new generation of followers.

Feng Shui is comparatively new to the West. The first reports of its existence appeared just over a century ago, from missionaries and consular officials working in the newly opened continent on the other side of the earth. Some of these people regarded it as superstitious nonsense, others as downright evil. All were puzzled as to how something so intangible, described as an 'influence upon the destinies of man', could be believed so wholeheartedly by what then amounted to one third of the world's population.

Chester Holcombe, an American consul in Peking, spoke for most of his fellow visitors when he wrote in *The Real Chinaman* (1895), 'This Feng Shui delusion holds the entire Chinese nation in subjection, and the professors of the art of divination

Living in Harmony: 'Mutual Agreement Influencing even the Dogs of the House', an engraving from an old Feng Shui commentary, *Shing Yu Seang Keae*.

are, as a class, as sincerely its victims as those who employ them to solve its tangled mysteries in their own affairs.' Constance Cumming, an intrepid English traveller, went even further in her *Wanderings in China* (1896): 'Feng Shui is a very nonsensical subject, but unfortunately it is one which throughout this Empire is a living reality, and one which is not only a bar to all scientific and material progress, but also often involves real danger and persecution to the promoters of Christian work.'

Even the name Feng Shui was baffling to these people: it was said to refer to the two elements of wind and water—the wind because no one fully understood it, and water because it could not be grasped. The nearest most foreigne~ ; got to translating it was 'the Astrology of the Earth'. But at least one Victorian tried to be fairminded about what he learned—F. S. Turner, a writer for the *Cornhill Magazine* in London, who concluded after a visit to Shanghai and Peking in 1874, 'This Chinese superstition, absurd as it may seem, has not maintained itself for a thousand years among a vast, civilised people, a nation whose thinkers and scholars are innumerable, without basing itself upon something or other natural to man and not evidently repugnant to his reason.'

Indeed, as subsequent research has shown, Feng Shui is the result of the profoundest thought and observation of the relationship between man and nature. It has been proved to be able to alter people's understanding about the world in which they live, as well as radically affecting their life-style. It can improve a person's home environment, his or her relationships with others and can even draw omens about the future. And it can work for you too.

In this book I have set out to explain the ancient knowledge of harmony between humans and nature which Feng Shui embodies, and to show how its systems for personal fulfilment can be made to work as effectively today as they first did in China at the dawn of that great and mysterious civilisation.

Philippa Waring
Singapore—Australia—England
1992–1993

風 水
1 WHAT IS FENG SHUI?

From the day Helen moved into her new London flat things seemed to go wrong. A normally vivacious and healthy girl, she became prone to bouts of sickness and felt listless and curiously ill at ease whenever she had to stay indoors for any length of time. Her natural energy and determination to get ahead in her career as a computer programmer also seemed to be sadly waning.

She had done her best to make the flat an attractive and comfortable place to live in. Even before she moved in, she had decorated the place from top to bottom—the living-room, bedroom, kitchen and bathroom—hung new curtains and arranged her furniture, several pieces of which were also new, to make the most of the limited space.

Yet, as the days turned to weeks and then months, first her optimism, then her work and finally the harmony of her life began to suffer. Indeed, it gradually began to dawn on her that something was fundamentally wrong with the flat *itself*. It just didn't feel right. She couldn't explain why, but the place was definitely having an adverse effect on her. How could she make this most crucial element in her life—her home—more wholesome to live in?

Helen found the answer in Feng Shui.

All she knew about this ancient Chinese art when it was recommended to her as the solution to her problems was that it claimed that the orientation and design of the rooms in which a person lived could have a profound affect on them. Feng Shui, she was told, maintained that a force of nature known as the 'breath of life'—which the Chinese had named *Chi*—circulated in every part of a building, rather like energy in the human body, and had to be allowed to flow smoothly or those living there would suffer. Thanks to the guidance she received from a Feng Shui expert (or *xiansheng*, as they are called), Helen was able to discover what was depressing the life energy in her new flat and improve it without either great effort or expense. And once she had done so, she found that her own energy, happiness and enthusiasm returned.

The problems with Helen's flat began right at her front door, for this faced directly onto a staircase, a conductor of bad *Sha*— the force which is said by the Chinese to oppose *Chi*. Yet by placing an ornamental screen just inside her doorway, she was able simply and effectively to counter this influence. In the living-room, she had innocently positioned her furniture in the form of an arrowhead because it looked stylish, and had put her television set in front of the windows. The lay-out of the chairs, said Feng Shui, was directing the harmful *Sha* straight into her bedroom opposite and doubtless interfering with her sleep; while the position of the TV created glare—another sign of *Sha*—and would affect her viewing. Simply by moving the television against an interior wall and rearranging the furniture, these trouble spots were eliminated.

In the kitchen, Helen had placed her refrigerator next to the central heating boiler and, according to Feng Shui, brought two opposing elements—fire and water—into contact, generating bad *Sha* in this room, too. Moving the fridge to a position adjacent to the sink—water beside water—enabled the balance to be restored. The table at which she worked faced towards a window and had to be re-orientated so that the light source was from the left.

In her bedroom, Helen had placed the bed directly parallel beneath a central beam that ran the length of the ceiling. Bad

Feng Shui, she was informed, and she was advised to move the bed away from the beam which was interfering with the flow of *Chi* through the room. It was also suggested that she should hang a lucky Chinese charm on the beam to counter its oppressive effect.

A change of colour scheme was suggested in the living-room to improve the Feng Shui, the red walls giving way to a more restful pastel green; while hanging a mirror on a wall at right-angles to the main window helped to deflect back outside the flat the bad *Sha* that was being generated by the buildings directly opposite.

Helen's introduction to Feng Shui proved a revelation: she had wondered how on earth a system, developed 3,000 years ago in rural China, could possibly have any relevance in modern London. These same thoughts were also shared by a young City businessman named Tom, who came to the conclusion that his home in the commuter belt of Surrey, to which he had moved less than a year before, was the reason for his declining fortunes.

Tom and his wife, Jill, had bought the house full of optimism. It was a detached, two-storey, three-bedroom property, situated on the edge of a five-year-old development of town houses. The fact that a railway line ran to the rear was certainly not ideal, but it had the advantage for Tom that he could step out of his front door and be on a London-bound train within five minutes. Twelve months later, however, the couple were seriously thinking of moving again, so unhappy had they become.

From being a close and loving partnership, Tom and Jill now frequently argued. Jill's health had suffered, and Tom's prospects of promotion had twice been dashed during the year. Tom knew he had not been giving as much attention to his work as in the past and put this down to the lethargy which had inexplicably taken hold of him since the move to the new house. Even the plans the couple had for the rather unprepossessing garden had been put aside as one problem seemed to pile on another.

They were on the point of deciding to sell up when Jill heard about Feng Shui. Tom, as he is now quick to admit, initially poured scorn on the very idea of some ancient Chinese superstition being of any use in their plight, and he was still sceptical when the changes suggested by an expert began to take effect.

The single worst factor affecting the house was its situation directly facing a T-junction, with the railway line at the rear further compounding the problem. The suggestion to counterbalance the road, which was responsible for directly channelling *Sha* through the front door, was to create a barrier in the form of a tree planted in a line with the road and the door; while at the rear, a line of poplar trees not only gave the house the protection it had previously lacked but screened off the railway, too.

Like Helen's flat in London, the interior of Tom and Jill's home harboured bad *Sha* in almost every room. The main staircase was positioned in line with the front door and was suspected of conducting any good *Chi* straight upstairs, to the detriment of all the ground floor rooms. In the bedroom the couple had positioned their bed directly facing the window which, as it faced west, let in too much light and (in the summer) heat, making undisturbed sleep difficult; while in the dining-room the main table was poorly illuminated and positioned too close to one of the walls, making it difficult to walk round. In the kitchen, the cooker and refrigerator stood side by side in a conflict of elements; while in Tom's study his desk— like Helen's table in her London flat—had been positioned under a window. All these defects were easily remedied by following the principles of Feng Shui: only the unfortunate juxtaposition of a lavatory next to the kitchen—which could channel bad *Sha* straight into the kitchen—proved difficult to counter. The recommendation of a bead curtain to halt the *Sha* offered probably the best solution.

The colour scheme of the house was assessed, and yellow— symbolic of wealth—was recommended in the living-room and study. Several ornaments symbolising long life and happiness were purchased to bring good luck into some of the other rooms.

The transformation in Tom and Jill's life after they allowed Feng Shui into their home proved as dramatic as it had been for

Helen. Tom's energy and sense of purpose were rekindled at home and soon became evident in his work where promotion followed. Jill's health was restored and she decided to take a new job. Together they set to and tackled the garden that they had so long neglected.

Those who have made a study of Feng Shui say that the stories of Helen and Tom and Jill are by no means unusual or isolated. All over the world, men and women who have followed the principles of Feng Shui, treating a home like a human body—its windows and doors the nose and mouth— and who have allowed the life energies to flow throughout, have been able to transform a 'sick' building into a healthy one.

Just how Feng Shui works, and how it can be made to work for you, are explained in this book.

*   *   *

The Chinese exponents of Feng Shui claim that *where* you live and *how* you allocate and arrange the rooms of your home can significantly influence the harmony of your life and your health, wealth and happiness. By taking advantage of the 'life energy' they call *Chi*, which flows everywhere, you can affect the whole tenor of your well-being.

These exponents believe that the orientation and design of your home has a major influence on the lives of all who live in it. The positioning of furniture, the direction in which a bed faces, the colour schemes and ornaments—all have a part to play in creating an environment that relaxes as well as stimulates the occupants. The simple act of rearranging a few chairs or changing a colour scheme can be highly beneficial—indeed, any number of misfortunes, from ill-health to financial problems and even marital break-ups, can be attributed to a house in which the principles of Feng Shui have been ignored or overlooked.

Feng Shui is also concerned with the location of the home, for its position in a neighbourhood may well be adversely influenced by the surroundings unless suitable countermeasures are taken to ward off the 'bad influences' of *Sha*. The flow of the essential life-giving forces, on the other hand, can be channelled to and from the premises by the position of adjacent buildings, roads, even hills and waterways.

A Feng Shui *xiansheng* I met in Singapore explained the basic purpose of the art to me.

'Most people are interested in how to succeed in life,' he said, 'and this is the type of advice in which modern Feng Shui specialises. It offers a code for regulating your life and a plan about where to live so that you can exploit your potential to the full.

'I happen to believe that Feng Shui is important for several reasons. It can make where you live special or meaningful, which in turn helps to foster a bond between a person and a place. It gives you an incentive to make your house into a real home, because good living conditions contribute to good health and these can lead to happiness, personal success and prosperity. It also reflects people's values and aspirations—and offers various rewards as well as warnings about the penalties of negligence. But what makes Feng Shui so fascinating is the fact that it has its mystical side as well as its practical side.

'Have you ever wondered why you feel more "at home" in one place than another? Why some houses always seem to bring bad luck to those who live there and no one feels at ease in them?

'It might have something to do with the way the place is built, of course,' he explained, 'or the neighbourhood in which it is built. Even the neighbours themselves. Our sense of comfort can also be affected by all sorts of things: congested spaces, barren landscapes, even ugly, badly proportioned buildings.

'There is no doubt that your relationship to your home is very important: it represents security and it also reflects your personality. Feng Shui believes that the environment in which we live affects the sort of people we are, and by balancing the two in harmony we can actually influence our future for the better.'

'Balance' and 'harmony' are two words heard constantly in any discussion of Feng Shui—for reasons that will become apparent as we explore further.

To understand the art of Feng Shui, 'the electricity of nature' as it has been described by some modern commentators, we need to appreciate the way natural science developed in China. Unlike the West, where the order of the day has always been to use practical tests and experiments when pursuing scientific discoveries, the ancient Chinese naturalists scorned the use of any instruments or tests. They did not dissect the bodies of animals or analyse organic substances, but recorded precisely what they *observed*, and in so doing they created a science that combines inner consciousness with ancient tradition and holds the powers of nature in the highest esteem.

These men first discovered the earth's natural energy forces centuries before orthodox science proved them to be the planet's magnetic field, and thereupon set about utilising them for the benefit of mankind. They stated that the 'breath of life', or *Chi*, flowed in wavering paths through the ground or along watercourses and could change direction as a result of any alterations made either by nature or by humans.

The ancient sages viewed the universe in which they lived as constantly changing and growing through the interaction of two continually moving forces: *Yin* which was female, dark, passive and negative, and *Yang* which was male, light, active and positive. These forces were not opposites, however, but formed a harmonious balance in which one could not exist without the other and together they pervaded all things, living and organic. The Chinese represented the forces of *Yin* and *Yang* by a curious symbol that looks rather like two identical tadpoles, one black and one white, entwined head to head.

The Yin and Yang symbol.

From their observations, the ancient sages also concluded that the earth's invisible energy forces were the same as those in the human body—what we call our 'energy'—and that just as the earth required the forces to be in perfect balance for the promotion of harmony and growth, so mankind needed a balance between mind and body in order to achieve good health and prosperity. Just as *Yin* must have its *Yang*, so the wavering force of *Chi* had its opposite in *Sha*—sometimes referred to in the earliest texts as 'the noxious wind' which could flow only in straight lines.

The harmony of Yin and Yang creates good Feng Shui—a Taoist sketch dated 1622.

In evolving the principles of Feng Shui and applying them in order to place humans in harmony with their environment, the early exponents discovered that the forces were universal and could be made to work wherever a person might live: in a city or a village, a mansion or a bedsit. Equally important, they learned how to balance the forces of *Chi* and *Sha*, showing how in the countryside the rivers and hills would channel the flow, while in towns and cities the same function was performed by buildings and roads.

There was no need to spend a lifetime looking for a Shangri-la somewhere on earth, they said: peace of mind—that great personal interior voyage of discovery—could be obtained through making the most of one's surroundings. Small wonder that such a system, which seeks to enhance the environment, should be seen by those who promote it to have a real relevance to today's ecological problems.

風 水
2 SEEKING THE IDEAL HOME

When it comes to the practical application of the ancient art of Feng Shui in the modern world, I cannot stress too emphatically that it is possible to utilise it just as effectively in the heart of a large city as in a sparsely populated rural area. Although the system may have been evolved at a time when the Chinese were largely free from the bureaucratic restrictions that control the siting of houses today, the principles laid down by the early exponents concerning the surrounding environment and the manner in which the beneficial *Chi* should be encouraged to flow around and through homes, whatever their size and locality, still apply equally well today.

The prime influences that affect the situation of every home and which must be taken into consideration in order to secure good Feng Shui for those who live there, are these:

1   *The Chi factor*: the 'breath of life' potential of the neighbourhood.
2   *The site orientation*: the importance of the direction in which a building faces.
3   *The five elements*: their influence upon a location.
4   *The power of water*: its significance in relation to a property.

Let us look at each of these factors in turn, beginning with the environment in which a building is situated.

1 THE CHI FACTOR

The Chinese sages who evolved Feng Shui were in no doubt that the 'breath of life' was the key to the harmonious existence they sought. To them it was the spirit that infused everything and gave it vitality: producing energy in mankind, giving life to nature, growth to plants, and movement to water. In order to exist, *everything* required *Chi*.

Once they had assured themselves about these natural forces, the wise men concluded that they must be positive (*Yang*) and negative (*Yin*) and devised a magnetic compass, the *Luopan*, to seek them out. I shall come to this instrument shortly.

Just as these invisible 'energy lines' existed in the earth, so they must flow in humans through the acupuncture meridians of the body. There had to be a perfect balance of the positive *Yang* and negative *Yin* elements of this energy in a human body to ensure good health, and in the earth for the production of vibrant *Chi*, the 'breath of life'.

Further study established that *Chi* came in various forms, consisting primarily of *Sheng Chi* (vigorous *Chi*) and *Ssu Chi* (inert or stagnant *Chi*). *Sheng Chi* was *Yang* while the torpid form was *Yin*, and it was believed that the former flowed most readily during the hours in which the sun was rising (from midnight to noon) while the latter predominated when the sun was declining in the afternoon and evening.

Yang and *Yin Chi* were also associated with the seasons, *Sheng Chi* being at its most active in the spring and summer months, and *Ssu Chi* operating in the autumn and winter. The omens in the first half of a month would also be better than in the latter, according to Feng Shui.

Chi can therefore clearly have a considerable effect on the timing of any Feng Shui project, spring and summer being ideal for major changes in life, especially when related to the home— either moving, renovating, or, most importantly of all, building a new house. As one of the early writers on Feng Shui, Hsaio Zhi, wrote in his book *Wu Xing Da Yi* around AD 600, 'Every year has twelve months, and each month has positions in time and space of vital and torpid *Chi*. Whenever one builds on a vital *Chi* position, wealth will accumulate; to violate a monthly position of torpid *Chi* will bring bad luck and calamity.'

Having established the nature of *Chi*, the need to locate it and take advantage of its power became the next priority of Feng Shui.

From their observations of the landscape all around them, the wise men came to several basic conclusions, the most important being that the best site of all for a house to take advantage of vital *Chi* was on a south-facing slope—ideally with a river running to one side of the building and then turning in front of it and disappearing underground.

Today we might argue that this is self-evident: any building on a south-facing slope gets the maximum hours of sunshine, is shielded from the north winds, and with its own river is provided with water for drinking and cleaning. By disappearing underground the river also carries away dirty water. But in fact a lot of what we call 'common sense' is to be found in Feng Shui.

The sages further concluded that for maximum benefit a building should be on a slope at the mid-point where two hills or mountains met, one slightly higher than the other. It was there, they agreed, that the magnetic currents in the earth, the positive and negative forces of *Yang* and *Yin*, also conjoined. They chose names for these two geographical formations: the Azure Dragon and the White Tiger.

In Chinese lore the dragon has always been considered superior to the tiger and hence it was important that the dragon hill should have greater prominence, be slightly higher and more rugged than its partner. The dragon formation also had to be on the tiger's left, and if the hills continued one behind the other, this was believed to create an even more propitious site, for it was symbolic of the two creatures mating.

Ernest J. Eitel, who wrote one of the first treatises on Feng Shui for Western readers, *Feng Shui; or, The Rudiments of Natural*

An ideal Feng Shui site created by the mountain shapes of the Azure Dragon and White Tiger—as drawn by a nineteenth-century Chinese *xiansheng*.

Science in China, which he published in 1873, explained the significance of the sites:

The symbolic Tiger and Dragon alliance which is the basis of Feng Shui.

The dragon and tiger are constantly being compared with the lower and upper portions of a man's arm, and in the bend of the arm the favourable site must be looked for. In other words, in the angle formed by the dragon and tiger, in the very point where the two (magnetic) currents which they individually represent cross each other—there is the luck-bringing site, the place to site a dwelling for the living or else a tomb where the dead may rest in peace.

In essence, he said, Feng Shui maintained that wherever there was an Azure Dragon hill there would be a smaller one representing the White Tiger, and together the pair would form a horseshoe shape. Any ridges along the hills would help direct the flow of the *Chi*, and the 'breath of life' would be at its most beneficial at the point where the two animal shapes conjoined.

A famous example of this principle in action is the Ming Tombs, known as the *Shi-san Ling* or Thirteen Tombs, situated to the north-west of Bejing, where the descendants of the Emperor Yung Lo were buried. The site was especially chosen because of its elongated amphitheatre of hills; the Emperor's own tomb stands in the centre of the horseshoe, while his descendants lie in graves scattered in similarly auspicious positions in the curves of the hills. The tombs are approached by an avenue of stone animals and courtiers, facing each other in pairs: camels and unicorns, elephants and horses, followed by pairs of civil and military officials.

A modern visitor to these tombs, who possesses even the most basic knowledge of Feng Shui, will probably not be surprised to learn that the hills to the east of the site are called the 'Azure Dragon Hill' while those to the west are known as 'White Tiger Hill'.

The guidelines for siting a more modest building for the living, in order to garner the *Chi* of a locality, were set down by a nineteenth-century Chinese Feng Shui *xiansheng* in a document which came into my possession during the research for this book. It is so rare to find written details of this ritual, so jealously do the native experts guard their secrets, that I feel it is well worth including here. The document, which is accompanied by an engraving of an expert at work on a site, takes the form of a question-and-answer dialogue between a client and a 'Dragon Man', as the Feng Shui experts are known in China.

QUESTION: When a man wishes to build a house according to Feng Shui, how does he go about it?

ANSWER: He purchases a plot of ground and, engaging a professor of geomancy to choose a lucky day, encloses the lot with a wall and prepares to lay the foundations.

Q: What are the ceremonies required in this work?

A: He must give public notice of his intentions, that all of his village may know, and all trouble from personal offence or interference be avoided. As to the height and depth of the house, there are fixed regulations to be observed. If, for instance, there is a high mountain behind, and a stream of water

The famous Ming Tombs near Beijing, burial place of the emperors, which were sited according to Feng Shui principles.

flowing in front, while on each side are ridges covered with trees, then the house should be from 20 to 30 feet high, with a tower, and extend back in six or seven courts or sections, and be from 50 to 60 feet broad to secure proper proportions.

Q: As to the surroundings, what should be done?

A: The professor of geomancy should examine the situation on all sides to see that there is nothing that would prove a hindrance to comfort or prosperity.

Q: In every village there are houses fronting in different directions—is this objectionable?

A: The lie of the land varies in different places. For instance, there may be a hill behind and level ground in front, but no outlying mounds or banks of gravel to flank the spot— then trees are planted to correct this defect. The houses are mostly on one plan, opening on the front and not at the side. If the hills behind form a semicircle and the wings of gravel bank extend for some distance, with broad fields between, in which clumps of trees, with springs of water, are found, there houses may be built facing each other from opposite sides of the plain.

Q: What are considered sources of evil in front of a house?

A: A straight road leading directly towards it, with people coming and going, or a small stream flowing in a straight course from it, are said to dissipate the good influences. To have the left side low and the right high are both unlucky signs. Feng Shui says that on the left is the Green Dragon and on the right the White Tiger, therefore whether it be a grave or a house the hills to the left should be higher than those to the right.

Q: Are there any means of rectifying defects in the situation?

A: If the left is low, plant trees to raise the height. If the water flows in too straight a course, make artificial bends and curves in it. If someone has built a house higher than yours, you can add to the height of your own, so that your view of the stars is not obstructed.

A Feng Shui *xiansheng* selecting the perfect site for a new dwelling. A Ching dynasty engraving.

2 THE SITE ORIENTATION

When it comes to selecting the ideal direction in which a house should face to take full advantage of the prevailing *Chi*, the south has always been the point most favoured by Feng Shui. Indeed, in order that they could locate the most suitable sites, the Chinese centuries ago devised their own special south-orientated compass which they named a *Luopan*. These direction finders, with their complex bands of symbols and characters, are normally only used now in advanced Feng Shui, when a house is being constructed from scratch on a virgin site, so it may be reassuring to know that for the purposes of this book an ordinary magnetic compass will serve just as well.

According to tradition, the basic Feng Shui compass, consisting of three rings centred round a magnetised needle, was devised some time during the seventh century, when its primary purpose was for determining the correct orientation of a new building or, more particularly, in selecting ideal sites for graves. Subsequent developments resulted in additional rings being added, so that today the most complicated *Luopan* can have anything up to 38 rings! The type most seen and used outside China, however, is the eight-ring compass illustrated on page 34.

The word *Luopan* divides into the syllables *lo*, meaning a spiral, and *P'an*, meaning a plate; and the compass is said to symbolise the radiation of goodness. It is approximately eight inches across, circular in shape to represent heaven, and made of lacquered wood rounded at the bottom like a saucer. The compass is covered with red and black Chinese characters and rests in the depression of a square board in which it is able to rotate. This base is said to be symbolic of the earth and is used when aligning the compass. The centre of the *Luopan* contains a small magnetised needle with a red end pointing to the south and the other, plain end seeking the north. This is known as the 'Heaven Pool' and the significance of the red end of the needle and its south orientation is important to understand.

Because of their ancient belief that they occupied the position of the 'Middle Kingdom' on the earth's surface and experi-

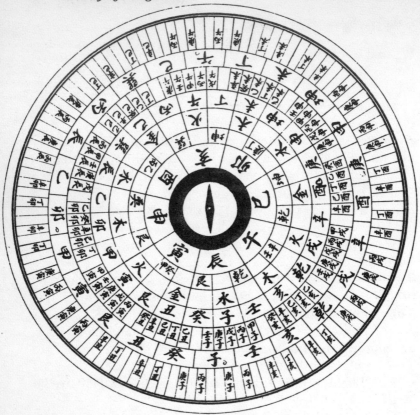

The *Luopan* compass used in the practice of Feng Shui always points to the south.

enced the greatest warmth and goodness coming from the south, the Chinese naturally enough aligned their compasses to the south. As most of their highest mountains were in the west and their rivers flowed eastwards, the east was placed on the left hand side of this cardinal point, with the west on the right. The north was simply a place from which the icy winds and darkness of winter came and hence took the lowest position. The early geomancers also added to these four points the names of appropriate creatures to symbolise the climatic conditions, as well as the four seasons in their appropriate locations— summer to the south, and so on. Their basic compass, therefore, looked like this:

⇑

SOUTH
(Red Phoenix: Warmth)
Summer

EAST   WEST

⇐ (Azure Dragon: Blue Seas)   (White Tiger: Snowy Mountains) ⇒

Spring   Autumn

NORTH
(Tortoise: Coldness)
Winter

⇓

It is important always to remember that when using a magnetic compass in place of a *Luopan* the readings as given on this diagram will be reversed.

3 THE FIVE ELEMENTS

Important though both the surrounding neighbourhood and direction of a building are believed to be in Feng Shui, more crucial still is a set of rules known as the 'Five Elements'. The importance of these lies in their interaction upon one another and the consequences which may result.

The five elements and their Chinese names are as follows:

WOOD: Mu
FIRE: Huo
EARTH: T'u
METAL: Chin
WATER: Shui

Curiously, although the Chinese have added wood and metal to the original list of elements devised by the Ancient Greeks—Fire, Air, Earth and Water—they omit what we have learned they value so highly, Air, namely Feng!

At the time Feng Shui evolved, Chinese astronomers believed that there were just five planets in the heavens, Jupiter,

Mars, Saturn, Venus and Mercury, and each of the 'Five Elements' was thought to be associated with a planet thus:

WOOD: Jupiter
FIRE: Mars
EARTH: Saturn
METAL: Venus
WATER: Mercury

However, it was the inter-relationship between the elements themselves which really concerned the early exponents of Feng Shui, as J. J. M. DeGroot, another of the early Western writers on the subject, explained in his book *The Religious System of China* (1897).

'These five elements,' he wrote, 'both produce and destroy each other if placed in certain conjunctions. Wood produces fire, fire produces earth, earth produces metal, metal produces water, water produces wood. On the other hand, metal destroys wood, wood destroys (i.e. absorbs) earth, earth destroys (i.e. absorbs) water, water destroys fire, fire destroys metal.'

Stated simply, the generation and destruction order of the Five Elements as laid down by Feng Shui can be shown in an order with which the reader should make himself familiar:

Order of Generation
WOOD
burns creating
FIRE
which leaves
EARTH
from which comes
METAL
that flows like
WATER
which grows
WOOD
and so on

Order of Destruction
FIRE
will melt
METAL
that chops down
WOOD
which draws goodness from
EARTH
that pollutes
WATER
which quenches
FIRE
and so on

These five Elements are also said to symbolise different degrees of *Yin* and *Yang*; five Cardinal Numbers; the four points of the compass plus the centre; as well as the seasons, weather conditions and the climate. Their symbolism and relationship are shown in the table on page 38.

Thus, by being able to classify everything into five categories, Feng Shui could ensure that the elements relating to any locality, building, or even inside a home, were in the right association one with the other. And if they were not, one could use countermeasures.

Once they had defined their Five Elements, the old sages were able to use each to categorise the different shapes of hills and mountains they observed round about, assigning elemental qualities to each:

1 *Peaked Mountain*

A majestic mountain which towers up to a narrow peak and is linked with the planet Mars and the Fire element.

ELEMENT	Wood	Fire	Earth	Metal	Water
YIN AND YANG	Lesser Yang	Greater Yang		Lesser Yin	Greater Yin
NUMBER	8	7	5	9	6
DIRECTION	East	South	Centre	West	North
COLOUR	green	red	yellow	white	black
SEASON	spring	summer		autumn	winter
WEATHER	wind	heat	sunshine	cold	rain
CLIMATE	windy	hot	humid	dry	freezing
PLANETS	Jupiter	Mars	Saturn	Venus	Mercury

2   *Rounded Mountain*

This similarly shaped feature which ends in a rounded top is identified with Jupiter and symbolises the element Wood.

3   *Squared Mountain*

A much squatter mountain which has a plateau on top and is linked with the planet Saturn and the Earth element.

4   *Curved Mountain*

This picturesque mountain which rises up to a softly curved summit is compared with the planet Venus and the element Metal.

5 *Cupola Mountain*

A more stunted mountain, with indentations on its summit containing watercourses, is associated with Mercury and the element Water.

Thus the Feng Shui sages knew from their list of conflicting elements whether mountains adjacent to one another were compatible or not, and whether they might be damaging to the *Chi* in the vicinity.

To take a typical example: a hill that represents Jupiter and the element Wood forms an unhappy alliance with one symbolising Mars and the element Fire. A striking instance of this particular conjunction exists in Hong Kong where the main peak fits the Jupiter definition while at its foot stands a hill known as Taipingshan which is symbolic of Mars. For many years it has been said that the most fires occurring anywhere in the Colony take place in Taipingshan!

We shall be returning shortly to the relevance of these shapes to a modern locality.

4 THE POWER OF WATER

Rivers, streams, lakes and pools—all forms of watercourses, in fact—are also an important factor in the ancient art: as the word *Shui*, meaning water, makes quite obvious. Interestingly, too, the Chinese word for *Chi* sounds very similar to that for 'stream'.

As I mentioned earlier, all watercourses are regarded as conductors of *Chi*. Consequently, those rivers which flow in curves or have a tortuous course are better able to direct the flow of *Chi* for the benefit of properties sited alongside them. These stretches of meandering waterway are often compared to the shape of the beneficial Azure Dragon. On the other hand, courses that run in straight lines or have sharp bends are much less propitious because they allow the *Chi* to 'run off' and dissipate like water.

The place where two watercourses meet can also be crucial in this context. If they join in a graceful curve, the *Chi* will be beneficial; but a confluence where the water is slowed up by silting or on the delta of a river will be unable to contain the *Chi*.

Water that flows quickly will conduct the *Chi* away from a locality, while a gently meandering stream conserves it and is highly desirable. The Chinese also say that a pool of water in front of a building is especially good at accumulating *Chi*—a clear indication of the value of a well sited garden pond!

The direction in which water flows in relation to a house is another factor to be borne in mind. The reason for this is that water is believed to be symbolic of wealth and status, both of which can 'flow' towards a home, either easily or with difficulty. In the words of another early Western commentator, John Edkins, writing in the *Chinese Recorder and Missionary Journal* in 1872, 'Riches and rank flow like water capriciously from one point to another. Hence riches and rank are supposed to depend on the undisturbed flow of the stream which passes in front of a site. And if due care is taken with the location, a perpetual stream of worldly honour and wealth may be expected to flow into the possession of the family.'

The most auspicious water course is certainly one that approaches a house directly from the east or west, especially if it is deflected around the building and then continues on its way in a lazy, meandering fashion. The suggestion here is that the *Chi* has been brought swiftly, but then lingers on as a result of the irregular course that follows.

If the watercourse lies to the south of the site, this is not a problem so long as the water is slow-moving and, as I shall explain, the exit is shielded in order that the *Chi* does not slip away rapidly.

The Chinese believe that a locality without water is ill-omened for it symbolises barrenness and can portend a lack of offspring for those families living in the immediate vicinity.

Despite such potential problems associated with water-courses, they do present an opportunity for the follower of Feng Shui to 'influence' his luck—for any stream or river can be subtly altered to capture the vital 'breath of life'.

To the Chinese who have engineered their water for centuries in order to irrigate their rice fields, such tasks come easily. In the West, however, drainage experts have always tended to straighten rivers or to channel water in direct lines.

For good Feng Shui, bends need to be introduced into straight rivers, sharp bends must be rounded and confluences should be created wherever possible. Indeed, some fine examples of the art in action can be seen in Hong Kong, where a number of formerly straight waterways close to large communities have been curved and several others diverted to form horseshoe-shaped moats—all intended to bring good luck to the local residents.

Such ideas are, of course, easier to explain than do in the West. Nevertheless, rivers still relentlessly pursue their inclination to erode new courses and a person fortunate enough to live near a stream possessing the right *Chi* can enhance its potential by planting suitable vegetation at the appropriate position on the bank to prevent the *Chi*'s sudden exit. Feng Shui does not demand confrontation with the Water Authorities to alter streams, rather a preservation of the timeless interaction between running water and the earth.

While water has undoubtedly been one of the main factors in shaping our landscape—cutting out mountains and valleys, levelling plains and shaping coastlines—the other equally important element is the wind which completes the equation *Feng* (wind) and *Shui* (water).

The ancient sages who devised Feng Shui visualised the *Chi* being carried on the winds as a result of their observation of smoke rising from candles and joss sticks. Studying the wafts and flurries as they rose into the air, they came to appreciate the working of convection currents long before this element of physics was made into a science in the West.

From their conclusions, they decided that if the wind was allowed to blow, uninterrupted, into a site from any direction, then its *Chi* would never have a chance to accumulate. And because the most hostile winds came from the north, so a house should be screened off from that direction by trees or some other form of protection. Conversely, because the warming and nurturing winds originated from the south, so that side of the property should be the most open, to allow easy access for the *Chi*.

The positioning of a property would never be quite perfect unless it was placed in a hollow, whether natural or man-made, where it was protected from any strong winds that might drive away all the good *Chi*. It was also important, though, that the building should not be so overshadowed in its hollow that the *Chi* would be unable to circulate, because, of course, stagnant *Chi* becomes *Sha*.

* * *

These, then, are the basic principles of Feng Shui. How to apply them to a typical Western city or town is the next stage in our search for the ideal home. This is where the importance of the 'Five Elements' and their interaction becomes apparent.

As we have seen, the ancient art compares each of these elements to a feature of the landscape: Fire to a pointed peak; Wood to a flat-topped mountain; Earth to a plateau; Metal to a rounded hill; and Water to a cupola-shaped mountain. These principles have to be applied to any modern landscape—and this can be done comparatively easily as you can see from the following examples:

- A rural location of undulating features or a town of buildings with uneven roofs can be said to be associated with the element WATER.
- A countryside dotted with tall trees and sharp hills or a

city dominated by church spires, factory chimneys or similar pointed buildings relates to the element FIRE.

- An unbroken, flat landscape or a community of solid, low-roofed properties, such as can be seen in many housing estates, is represented by the element EARTH.
- Rolling hills and forests or man-made structures such as office blocks, tall apartment buildings, even bridges and viaducts, are related to the element WOOD.
- A rounded landscape or a town of buildings with curved or arched roofs is associated with the element METAL.

Now, using the table opposite as a guide, you should be able to compare the outline of your property against the shape of the neighbourhood to find out whether or not they are compatible and will therefore encourage or discourage the flow of *Chi* towards your own home.

A classic example of compatibility would be a steep-roofed house indicative of FIRE in a landscape where WOOD predominated, for wood is the prime requisite of fire and would nurture the home, making it a happy place to live in. Because fire also represents ambition, such a neighbourhood would especially suit anyone with a 'burning' desire to succeed.

On the other hand, a landscape in the shape of WATER, where the buildings have the form of WOOD, would nourish growth at a less hectic pace and would be ideal for those who put relationships and happiness above material possessions, while a property categorised as METAL would clearly be ill-omened in a FIRE neighbourhood.

Feng Shui attaches further symbolism to each of the 'Five Elements', which is also well worth bearing in mind when selecting a home:

- WOOD is said to signify growth and creativity and would be ideal for those contemplating starting a family or working from home.
- FIRE is very much associated with intellectual development and achievement and would make a good base for high flyers.
- EARTH, being symbolic of bricks and mortar, suggests

BUILDING SHAPE	ENVIRONMENT				
	Fire	Wood	Earth	Metal	Water
FIRE apartment blocks, sharp roofs	stable, but short-term	prosperity	happiness and achievement	social success	ill-omened
WOOD flats, sky-scrapers	danger of upheaval	very stable	beneficial in short-term	hazardous tenancy	harmony and growth
EARTH Estates, flat roofs	continuity and stability	lack of stimulation	stability	peaceful and retiring	success but isolation
METAL Large properties, domed roofs	financial problems	loneliness and anxiety	prosperity	stability	unspectacular progress
WATER Detached houses, irregular structures	unhappy relationship with neighbours	harmonious living	environmental pollution	prosperity and good fortune	stability and flexibility

endurance and reliability and would make an excellent
environment for the commuter.

* METAL is said to be symbolic of money, and dwellings
  with domed roofs are highly suitable for those hoping to
  achieve financial success in banking or commerce.
* WATER is seen as ever changing and has always been
  regarded by the Chinese as the element of
  communication—hence it provides an ideal environment for those in the media: advertising, the press, films,
  TV and so on.

Interestingly, buildings which have a lot of glass in their
construction are said to belong to the Water element, although
some Feng Shui experts insist that the glass towers which are
now increasingly dominating our cities are actually a combination of the Water and Earth elements which, of course, are said
to be in opposition to one another!

However, if you are already living in a property where the
elements are in opposition—or indeed are contemplating
moving to one which suits your needs in all other respects—
Feng Shui says it is quite possible to alleviate the situation by
introducing what is known as a 'Controlling Element'.

I have already explained the Generation and Destruction
sequence of the Five Elements on pages 36–7, but it would
probably be as well to show them here again in the form of
simple diagrams. Remember that where the elements are
generating one another, then those which are adjacent *help* each
other; while in the destructive sequence they will *destroy* their
neighbours.

A 'Controlling Element' is one that either 'destroys' the
element causing the harm or alternatively 'regenerates' the one
under threat. To take a simple example: if a WOOD property
such as a flat is under threat in a hazardous METAL environment, then the introduction of a controlling element of
WATER will generate WOOD, while the employment of FIRE
will destroy the METAL. The table on page 48 gives a list of the
Controlling Elements that are to be used in opposition to each
of the threatening elements.

GENERATION

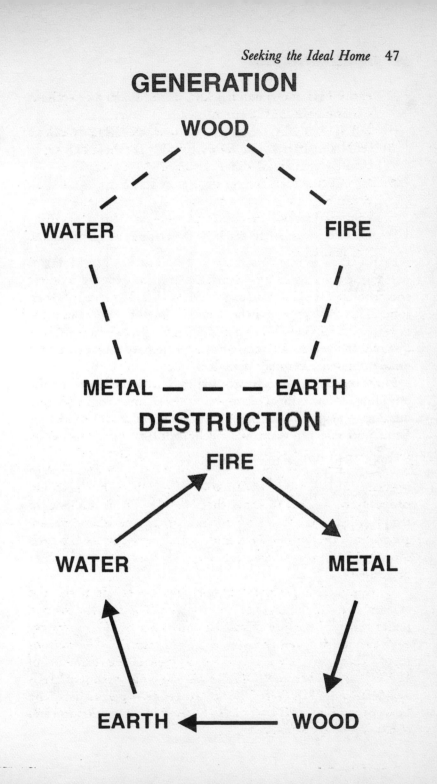

DESTRUCTION

THE CONTROLLING ELEMENTS

BUILDING SHAPE	THREATENING ELEMENT	CONTROLLING ELEMENTS	
		Creative	Destructive
FIRE	Water	Wood	Earth
WOOD	Metal	Water	Fire
EARTH	Wood	Fire	Metal
METAL	Fire	Earth	Water
WATER	Earth	Metal	Wood

Over the years, the Feng Shui experts have suggested many different everyday items which contain the necessary controlling elements to be utilised in the protection of a building. A few typical examples of those most commonly used may help to make the table clearer and enable you to put it into effect in your own circumstances.

- FIRE: Where the landscape consists of sharp roofs, WATER is the required element and an ornamental pond in the garden, or a water container or pot plant in the window of a flat, will counter the effect.
- WOOD: A landscape of tall buildings, lamp posts, telegraph poles and trees requires the counter-effect of METAL, and a goldfish in a bowl represents both metal and fire.
- EARTH: The flat roofs of estates require the counter-influence of WOOD and the planting of trees or a green colour scheme for the property; alternatively, indoor plants on a window sill will curb the problem.
- METAL: Where there are large domed properties, FIRE will be the controlling element to put into effect, and the use of the colour red as a decoration, or alternatively lights, candles or other forms of illumination in the windows should suffice.

- WATER: In landscapes of irregular buildings EARTH is the controlling element, and the use of stone figures in the garden or ceramic bowls or vases in the windows will provide protection.

Of course, it is quite possible that a building may be under threat from more than one element, in which case both the generative and destructive factors will have to be employed. Below are listed some more everyday items recommended to me by a *xiansheng* in Singapore, which he maintained actually embody dual elements and can be used either in the garden of a house or in the window of an apartment to counter the problems.

FIRE and WOOD: Red garden flowers, an incense burner.
FIRE and EARTH: Outdoor lamp made of pottery, table oil lamp.
FIRE and METAL: Red porcelain garden ornament, silver candelabra.
FIRE and WATER: Central heating system, pyramid glass jar.
WOOD and EARTH: Cactus garden, dried plants in a vase.
WOOD and METAL: Green-painted garage, wooden-handled knife or sword.
WOOD and WATER: Garden pond with aquatic plants, decorative bamboo pipe.
EARTH and METAL: Iron container of sand, gold or brass ornaments.
EARTH and WATER: Ornamental water fountain, display of seashore pebbles.
METAL and WATER: Iron bird bath, metal-framed painting of a water scene.

You should bear in mind that those who practise Feng Shui as a profession in the Chinese communities of the world vary their guidance very considerably when defining what the counter-elements must be in any given situation. The examples I have given can therefore only be taken as a general guide, but they will still materially contribute to the flow of *Chi* to any property.

*   *   *

Once you have established the suitability of the neighbour-hood, the property itself can be considered in Feng Shui terms.

As we have seen, in the ancient Chinese world where the art first evolved, the wise men decided that the ideal position for a house was on a south-facing slope protected against the en-croachment of *Sha* from the rear (north) by hills forming a horseshoe shape in which the Azure Dragon (to the east) was more prominent than the White Tiger on the western side.

Now although features such as these might be easily recog-nisable in hilly and mountainous regions, nothing similar was apparent on the vast open plains of China. So the Feng Shui *xiansheng* decreed that the requisite 'protection' to all south-facing properties could be provided either by erecting an undulating wall or by planting a line of trees to the north of a building. These artificial substitutes must not be so large or so close to the house as to obscure the sunlight and disrupt the flow of *Chi*. These guidelines are, of course, still applicable today.

With the rise of civilisation and the growth of towns and cities, however, it soon became obvious that it was not possible for everyone to find the perfect situation, and consequently the wise men devised a system of orientation that could be applied to any locality. It involved, first, the use of the *Luopan* to establish the compass direction, and, secondly, the creation of a table of orientation for potential occupants, drawn up by the sages from their observation of the planetary system.

The Orientation Table was based on the year of a man's or woman's birth and suggested the ideal direction in which that person should orientate his or her home. If the front door already faced in the required direction, this was ideal, but if not, the compass direction was to be used as a general guide to the orientation of the front entrance in relation to the main rooms—the living-room and the bedroom, the two prime centres through which the 'breath of life' must be encouraged to flow smoothly.

The table, which is reprinted opposite, has been amended to cover twentieth-century birth dates, and will enable anyone who lives in a house or flat where the direction of the property is

ORIENTATION TABLE

Women

SE	E	SW	N	S	NE	W	NW	NW
1908	1907	1906	1905	1904	1903	1902	1901	1900
1917	1916	1915	1914	1913	1912	1911	1910	1909
1926	1925	1924	1923	1922	1921	1920	1919	1918
1935	1934	1933	1932	1931	1930	1929	1928	1927
1944	1943	1942	1941	1940	1939	1938	1937	1936
1953	1952	1951	1950	1949	1948	1947	1946	1945
1962	1961	1960	1959	1958	1957	1956	1955	1954
1971	1970	1969	1968	1967	1966	1965	1964	1963
1980	1979	1978	1977	1976	1975	1974	1973	1972
1989	1988	1987	1986	1985	1984	1983	1982	1981
1998	1997	1996	1995	1994	1993	1992	1991	1990

Men

SW	E	SE	SW	NW	W	NE	S	N
1908	1907	1906	1905	1904	1903	1902	1901	1900
1917	1916	1915	1914	1913	1912	1911	1910	1909
1926	1925	1924	1923	1922	1921	1920	1919	1918
1935	1934	1933	1932	1931	1930	1929	1928	1927
1944	1943	1942	1941	1940	1939	1938	1937	1936
1953	1952	1951	1950	1949	1948	1947	1946	1945
1962	1961	1960	1959	1958	1957	1956	1955	1954
1971	1970	1969	1968	1967	1966	1965	1964	1963
1980	1979	1978	1977	1976	1975	1974	1973	1972
1989	1988	1987	1986	1985	1984	1983	1982	1981
1998	1997	1996	1995	1994	1993	1992	1991	1990

other than south-facing to arrange, or rearrange, the interior in such a way as to satisfy Feng Shui. Unless you are very unlucky, no structural changes should be necessary.

To use the table, first check the precise direction in which the property faces by means of a compass (if you do not have a *Luopan*) and establish the south point. Then, referring to the columns, find your birth date. The orientation that is applicable to you will be at the top of that column. For example, if, like me, you were born in 1944, your orientation is south-west.

Even though you may not be able to alter the direction in which your home faces, you can control the internal space to your advantage, changing the function of one room to another in order to enhance the *Chi* factor. Indeed, even in a one-room flat, by ensuring that the bed and living space occupy the appropriate section of the area and the parts for cooking and washing are well away from these, Feng Shui is satisfied. In the next chapter I shall discuss in more detail how to utilise and arrange the interior rooms of your home.

To end this chapter, it may be helpful to mention a few general rules that Feng Shui has associated with properties in general.

The importance of water in the vicinity of a house has already been mentioned, especially watercourses that arrive from one side of the property, turn in front of it, and then disappear shortly afterwards. This situation exists in London's Docklands, which is one of the reasons why the resident Chinese population believe the area to be a favourable spot to live in! If the water does not go underground, Feng Shui says this requirement can be satisfied by screening the river as it passes the boundary with a small brick wall, a hedge or some shrubs.

In properties that back on to a river, Feng Shui says that the entrance must be at the rear to allow the *Chi* to gain entrance. If the ground slopes upwards from the front of a building, then the entrance should again be at the back. Properties facing open space to the south—particularly a valley, a tract of land such as a heath, or even the sea—are ideal because of the gentle winds that come from the south and allow the beneficial *Chi* to enter unhindered.

A house on a triangular plot of land is said to be ill-omened because the odd shape will attract *Sha*, although if the front door is on the side of the triangle rather than at the point, this counters the effect. Similarly, a house facing a T-junction or at the end of a cul-de-sac will be on the receiving end of the straight-moving flow of *Sha*—as well as in the direct line of all the street noise! A dead-end street not only 'traps' bad *Sha* but gives its residents the feeling of being trapped, too.

The Chinese have always believed that a house in which the front is slightly lower than the back is well suited to disperse the influence of *Sha*, but such properties are not a normal feature in Western architecture. Similarly, a house with a large tree immediately opposite the front door is said to be ill-omened, as this will 'deflect' the entrance of money.

It should be clear from this that other buildings and man-made features around a property can also affect the flow of *Chi* and must be carefully borne in mind. In a built-up area, the relationship of your home to other properties is important, especially if the corner of another building, such as a block of flats or a terrace of houses, 'points' at it. According to Feng Shui, all sharp angles such as this are known as 'Secret Arrows' and can direct the harmful *Sha* straight into your house. They are said to create an unhealthy environment in which illness is often present.

These sharp angles can be even more unlucky on office buildings—for while curves will attract money, straight edges drive it away. An example of this principle in action, quoted to me by a Feng Shui expert, is the angular new Lloyd's Building in Lime Street, London, which, of course, has been 'hit' by a number of huge losses since it was opened.

On the other hand, the flat edges of buildings which lead towards the front of your property are good conductors of *Chi*— although if there is a road in front which turns at a right angle this can bring about the same effects as the 'Secret Arrows'. A driveway up to the front door should always be laid out in a gentle sweep, to waft in the good influences.

I have already referred to the effect that a tree situated in front of the door can have on a family's prosperity. In fact all obstructions of this kind are ill-omened: lamp posts, telegraph poles, power lines, even monuments and columns are said to conduct *Sha* into the building. Pylons, tall chimneys and storage tanks can have the same effect if the property lies in their shadow. Fortunately, with so many of the utilities laying their wires underground and street lights being attached to buildings or suspended overhead nowadays, these risks are being minimised.

Railway tunnels, road cuttings, bridges and other similar features which run towards a property are also to be avoided, although the intervention of watercourses such as ponds, reservoirs and canals can cancel out the effect of the *Sha*. The best conductors of *Chi* are, invariably, natural features which lack the hard lines of man-made constructions—with rock formations, uneven groups of trees and irregular shapes on the horizon being the natural blocks to the *Sha*.

All neighbourhoods have their own distinctive features which can be recognised with careful observation and, armed with this information, Feng Shui endeavours to help you find the place that is most suitable for you to live in. Using the guidelines I have outlined, it should be possible to establish which elements (if any) are in opposition to one another in your neighbourhood, or are directly affecting your building, and to introduce the necessary controlling elements listed on page 48.

Once you have completely grasped these important factors of Feng Shui and can appreciate how they function in the neighbourhood around a building, you will be in a position to set about ensuring a plentiful flow of *Chi* into the heart of your home—its interior rooms—with confidence.

風 水

3 THE DOOR TO HAPPINESS

For many people, the interior of their home is the most important aspect of their lives, the one upon which they most wish to
bring to bear the benefits of Feng Shui. The selection of the
most suitable rooms for the different functions of their lives, the
décor and the arrangement of furnishings are viewed as the
primary function of the art—a belief very much in keeping with
that of the exponents who devised it so many years ago. And
there is no doubt that, with the proper attention to the interior
details, the most unfavourable elements inside *and* outside a
home can be overcome and the lives of those living there
transformed.

The ancient Chinese may never have heard the expression
'an Englishman's home is his castle', but their intention to
make their homes conducive to harmonious living had precisely the same intent. To them, a house was just like a body
that needed to 'breathe' the good influences of *Chi* through its
doors and windows to ensure good health.

To some Westerners unaware of its subtleties, household
Feng Shui may seem at first glance rather like a mixture of
common sense and good taste—a kind of 'mystic interior
design', I have heard it called—and certainly the correct use of
colour, lighting and furnishing in a home is a primary factor in

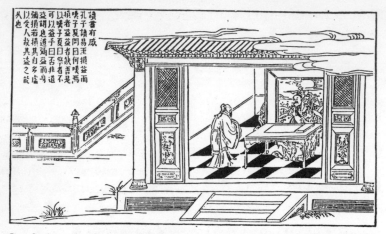

Confucius, the famous Chinese sage, was a student of Feng Shui.

creating a person's state of well-being. A room decorated in warm colours undoubtedly makes those in it feel warmer, just as subdued lighting relaxes them and the right décor puts them at their ease. Nor would anyone deny that superior living conditions are an important element in good health which, in turn, can inspire success and prosperity in all aspects of life.

But to the followers of Feng Shui there is much more to it than that. Why, they ask, will a person feel more at home in one place than another? It is certainly not pure chance, but the fact that the man or woman is *in tune* with the surroundings. For the art shows us that everything contains living organisms and everything has its own environment and conditions in which it exists best—not the least of these 'organisms' being the human race. But unlike most other organisms, we can choose our situation and indeed manipulate it to enhance our harmony.

As we have seen, the Chinese learned centuries ago that living in tune with nature and the energy of the earth was the secret of this state of household bliss. They demonstrated, too, how this energy could be detected and used to encourage the beneficial forces of *Chi* and deflect those of *Sha*. The sum achievement of this was a living environment—even one sur-rounded by hostile man-made or natural forces outside its walls—that would satisfy mankind's deepest need for a secure and comfortable home. It was a system flexible enough to work anywhere.

THE OMENS OF NUMBERS

Before stepping through the door of what you want to be a happy home, it is as well to note that Feng Shui says that even the numbers of houses are important—and not just because the Chinese language is so well adapted to puns, as I have heard some sceptics claim! In geomantic terms, the numbers 2,5,6,8,9 and 10 are lucky, while numbers 1,3 and 4 are unlucky. The reasons for this are as follows:

- 2 indicates the achievement of things easily.
- 5 is linked to the propitious 'Five Elements'.
- 6 is symbolic of wealth.
- 8 is an omen of becoming wealthy.
- 9 is the sign of long life.
- 10 is an indication of a 'certainty'.

On the other hand, the other numbers are unlucky for these reasons:

- 1 is an unpopular number because of the Chinese belief in the duality of Yin and Yang.
- 3 is similarly ill-omened because it is an odd number, although in Chinese it actually sounds very like the word for 'alive'.
- 4 is deemed to augur bad luck because it enunciates just like *si*, meaning death.

Feng Shui maintains that good fortune is attached to properties with dual numbers because a single number can be an omen of loneliness. Care should always be taken, however, where the address contains several digits, because applying the symbolism of the numbers can produce some surprising results. For example, 28 signifies 'easy to become rich' while 104 spells out 'certainty to die'.

Small wonder, then, that estate agents in Chinese communities all over the world have reported instances of clients haggling for weeks over prices in order to avoid a total that contains ill-omened numerals. Some have even had two identical houses for sale with the numbers 4 and 8 and been unable to find a Chinese client who will even look at the first property!

THE POWER OF MIRRORS

Now to some general points regarding the home itself. In China, many houses have a little wall built across the front door a short distance away from it, as a barrier to the *Sha*. These walls are known as *Ying Pei* (Spirit Screens) and are probably the best known manifestations of Feng Shui. They are hardly applicable in the West, however, where other alternatives have had to be devised by the *xiansheng*.

Wherever possible the front door should open inwards to allow the beneficial *Chi* to enter. The back door, on the other hand, should open outwards so that after the vital energy has wafted gently through each room via the passageways and staircases it can disperse. If it is not possible to re-hang doors in order to satisfy these rules, the *Chi* can still be attracted through the front door by a number of alternatives.

Throughout the Far East, I saw innumerable examples of Feng Shui in action through the affixing of good luck symbols to ill-omened doors. These included brass symbols of dragons and metal door-knockers in the horseshoe shape representative of the Azure Dragon/White Tiger alliance. I was assured that the familiar western horseshoe could be used equally effectively. In many Chinese homes, too, one of the familiar wind chimes hanging in the doorway, or a painting of a tiger on a wall near the front door, are said to help dispel evil influences.

At the rear of the property, the stagnant air can be encouraged to leave through a door that opens inwards by hanging an ordinary household mirror on the wall immediately inside so that, when opened, it reflects the garden or landscape outside and directs the 'noxious fumes' out. I shall elaborate further in a moment on the importance of mirrors in Feng Shui. Where the back door is under threat from *Sha*, then ideally a small wall such as the *Ying Pei* might be erected in the garden opposite the door.

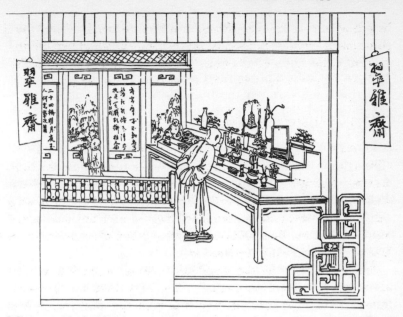

Mirrors, wind chimes and other Feng Shui artefacts on sale in a
Singapore curiosity shop, circa 1900.

Any house which has a central passageway running from the
front door to the back—or at least one where the back door is
visible from the front—will not enjoy good Feng Shui without
remedy, for such an arrangement will allow access of the
harmful *Sha* energy and quickly conduct out any good *Chi*. In
this context, it has been suggested that couples who occupy
separate rooms divided by a straight corridor are seriously
endangering their relationship for this can 'cut off' their love.

Most experts are agreed that the best and simplest method of
preventing good *Chi* from travelling straight into and out of a
home which has entrances and exits in alignment is to place a
small partition or screen in the hallway just behind the front
door. A net curtain hanging from the door frame can be equally
beneficial. The ideal hallway should also not be too narrow,
although if it is, always ensure that it is brightly lit so as not to
dampen the *Chi*, nor, indeed, the mood of the owner the
moment he or she arrives home!

Feng Shui also says that to have the front gate on the same

alignment as the front door will quickly disperse the house's good luck. Similarly, the current Western taste for combined sitting- and dining-rooms running the whole length of a property, with windows at each end, is not conducive to *Chi*—which can thus pass through the building without having time to meander and disperse its life-enhancing energy.

Here again it is important to slow the *Chi* down. In the case of a front gate aligned to a front door, the introduction of a small curve in the path will have the desired effect, and should not be too difficult to achieve by even the most modest gardener. Where a single room runs the length of a house, positioning items of furniture such as bookshelves, a cocktail cabinet or even a stereo system between the sitting and dining areas will have sufficient effect to redirect the *Chi*.

Chinese followers of Feng Shui have always been against having staircases running up directly behind the front door, as this causes the *Chi* to pass to the first floor without having circulated on the ground level. The ideal staircase is one towards the rear of the building, on a side wall, and with a landing or change of direction halfway up.

In most cases it is not possible to change the position of a staircase which conflicts with this guideline. I have, however, seen it most effectively countered in Chinese homes by hanging a curtain across the bottom of the stairs—which also, of course, acts as a good draught excluder against any cold air coming in through the front door!

A simple method of checking whether the *Chi* can circulate through any building is to walk from the front entrance through every room of the house, entering and leaving each one by a different door—if possible avoiding recrossing your own path before reaching the back door.

Clearly, while such an arrangement might be possible in a house being built from scratch, in the average modern Western home many rooms only have a single door. The answer to this problem in many cases will be the ubiquitous mirror whose use I have already described at the back door.

It is important always to bear in mind that, according to Feng Shui, the function of a mirror in the home is not simply for the making of human reflections. For centuries the Chinese have considered it even more important in assisting the beneficial *Chi* to continue on its way when it is in danger of reaching a dead end. Therefore the angle at which a mirror hangs is crucial. It should be face-on to the potentially dangerous spot so that the *Sha* is reflected back on itself and out of the building. Ideally, a mirror should reflect a harmonious scene from the outside, like trees or water.

Where it proves impossible to hang a mirror in such a way that it can divert the *Chi*, a lucky charm such as chimes, or the *Yin* and *Yang* symbol hung from the ceiling in front of the doorway, should prove a satisfactory solution. Later we shall be considering the efficaciousness of various charms and talismans.

Mirrors are especially important in any enclosed or windowless room, such as a bathroom or lavatory, for without one these places become what are known in Feng Shui terminology as 'Dead Areas', and can prove a hazard to the health of the occupants. Indeed, mirrors are so widely used by the Chinese to overcome bad Feng Shui that it is not surprising to hear some Western exponents of the art describe them as 'the aspirin of Feng Shui'!

I shall be coming to the factors affecting the individual rooms of the house shortly, but it is worth mentioning here that in general terms Feng Shui believes that people who live and work in rooms where there is plenty of *Chi* are energetic, enterprising and likely to be successful in their objectives. Some experts claim that the *Chi* often centres in the living-room, but all *xiansheng* are agreed that it is most important that it should circulate freely in the bedroom.

The Chinese have always believed that the bedroom is the place where life is refreshed and reinvigorated, and where this room is situated in relation to the rest of the house is therefore important. To help in making this choice, Feng Shui offers the assistance of a group of very ancient symbols known as the 'Eight Trigrams' which are said to embody all the wisdom of the universe. Each of these signs has been assigned to a point of the compass (the primary points being supplemented by the intermediaries North-East, South-East and so on) and a member of the family. When the trigrams are then used in conjunction with a plan of a house they will determine in which quarter of the house each member of the household should sleep in order to take full advantage of the incipient *Chi*.

Before explaining how the Eight Trigrams operate, however, we need to look at their evolution.

THE EIGHT TRIGRAMS

According to Chinese tradition, it was the very first ruler of the nation, Emperor Fu Hsi, who lived around 2953–2838 BC, who discovered these immortal symbols while he was studying the markings on the back of a tortoise, one of China's sacred animals. As a result they are now regarded as being among the most sacred emblems in Chinese history.

The tradition states that the combinations of solid and broken lines that the Emperor saw on each of the eight panels of the creature's shell encapsulated all the knowledge of the universe—a knowledge, the sages say, that can only be understood by those able to interpret their meanings. Small wonder the trigrams have come to be held in the highest esteem throughout the East (in South Korea, for example, they form part of the country's national flag).

Such grand claims made about the trigrams are, however, somewhat difficult to appreciate when first looking at their unprepossessing appearance. They derive from the ancient principles, *Yin* and *Yang*: the male element indicated by a solid line and the female by one broken in the middle. Each trigram consists of three horizontal lines, which in all the different combinations allows for eight separate permutations to be constructed.

These trigrams can then be combined together in pairs to form hexagrams of six lines. And when these six lines have been paired in all their possible permutations a grand total of 64 hexagrams results.

Quite who first thought out all these permutations we do not know—although Emperor Fu Hsi must surely be a favourite candidate for he is known to have used the Eight Trigrams in Feng Shui for casting horoscopes, as we shall see in Chapter 6—but in about 1143 BC a certain King Wen systemised the 64 hexagrams, gave them names, and added interpretative texts to each. Further deciphering was done by the king's son, the Duke of Chou, who added notes to help explain the meaning of each. From their work came what we now know as the *I Ching*, or Book of Changes, which has been called 'one of the world's most revered works of fortune telling' according to numerous sources.

The great Confucius later added some further notes to the book, but for all this study it has remained a puzzling work, full of symbolism and hidden meanings, which demands that the reader use his own powers of interpretation and imagination to unlock the secrets of the ancient wisdom it contains. This is no easy task—as Confucius himself remarked after years of study, when he was 70 years old.

'If some years were added to my life,' he declared, 'I would give fifty to the study of the *I Ching* and might then escape falling into great errors.'

But to return to the Eight Trigrams and their connection with Feng Shui. Each has a Chinese name which, to Western ears, may sound curiously similar. They are formed by drawing a solid or broken line, beginning, as is the Chinese fashion, with the bottom line and moving upwards. Those with the solid line or lines at the bottom are said to portend stability, while the broken lines indicate movement and change. Here are the eight trigrams:

CH'IEN: Three solid lines: pure Yang

SUN: A single Yin line below two Yang lines

LI: A Yin line between two Yang lines

KEN: Two Yin lines beneath a Yang line

TUI: Two Yang lines below a Yin line

K'AN: A Yang line between two Yin lines

CHEN: A Yang line beneath two Yin lines

K'UN: Three broken lines: pure Yin

Simple as these lines undoubtedly appear, to believers in Feng Shui they embody a wealth of experience distilled over the centuries, regarding the attainment of harmony, prosperity and romance. Equally, they are crucial in selecting the sleeping quarters for members of the family.

As the first step to understanding how the trigrams are applied to bedrooms, the illustration opposite shows how each has been allotted to a compass point:

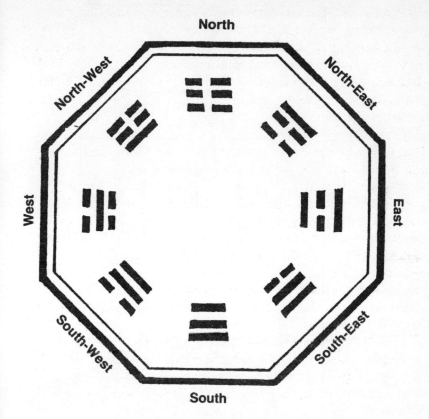

Apart from their links with the compass points and the individual members of the family, Feng Shui says that the trigrams are also associated with specific qualities, elements and symbolism which can most easily be summarised by the chart on page 66.

By referring this chart to a ground plan of any house, flat, even a bed-sit, it is possible to establish the most suitable location for the sleeping area of any particular member of a family. You will, of course, be immediately struck by the fact that the husband and wife are shown at directly opposite sides of the compass and, by inference, in rooms at opposite ends of the house. You have to appreciate that when Feng Shui was evolved, Chinese couples had their own rooms to which they

Trigram	Family Member	Element	Quality	Symbolism
Ch'ien (S)	Father	Metal	Strength	Heaven
Tui (SE)	Youngest Daughter	Metal	Happiness	Sea
Li (E)	Middle Daughter	Fire	Brightness	Heat
Chen (NE)	Eldest Son	Wood	Vigour	Thunder
K'un (N)	Mother	Earth	Nourishment	Earth
Ken (NW)	Youngest Son	Earth	Obstacles	Mountain
K'an (W)	Middle Son	Water	Movement	Fluid
Sun (SW)	Eldest Daughter	Wood	Wind	Growth

could retire to rest, dress or carry out their toilet needs, but it was the husband's room in which they *slept*. In using the compass and the room chart for Feng Shui today, it should also be taken as read that the south-facing room is the one best suited for the head of the household—whether this is a man or a woman, a couple or a single person.

In more general terms, Feng Shui states that it is not advisable for two bedrooms to be connected as this takes away the independence of the occupiers. Nor should bedrooms be built over empty spaces such as garages or store rooms, for these create a *Chi* vacuum.

ROOMS WITH A VIEW

The ancient wise men who collected the basic principles of Feng Shui also provided some useful guidance from their studies about the use to which any other unoccupied rooms of a property might be put. Once again, the following table summarises this aspect of Feng Shui for easy reference:

DIRECTION GUIDE

Room	Good Chi
Front Entrance	South
Staircase	South-East
Dining-room	East or South-East
	South or South-West
Sitting-room	West
Study	East or West
Bathroom	North
Toilet	North
Bedroom	South
Garage	North

As will be evident from this chart, the North is the ill-omened location for the majority of rooms, a situation which is difficult for many Western households to overcome. Therefore Feng Shui advises that the furnishings which are put into such a room are all orientated slightly away from the northerly direction—North-East or North-West—as this will neutralise the bad *Sha*.

Feng Shui favours lots of doors and windows in a home, regarding these as the orifices which allow the *Chi* to circulate freely—not to mention providing good ventilation for the occupants. However, any room with too many doors is likely to disperse the energy as well as being a draughty place for the occupants.

Doorways and window sills can be important in deflecting the 'Secret Arrows' caused by the corners of adjoining buildings or street junctions. Here the placement of favourable items such as an evergreen plant or a statue in the window, or a musical chime in the doorway, will prevent the *Sha* from entering.

Often in Chinese households a bamboo flute will be found hanging just inside the door—and as the word for flute in Chinese sounds almost exactly the same as 'disappear', the significance is obvious!

Windows themselves can be extremely helpful in preventing the *Sha* entering a home if they are used as the focal point for positioning 'controls' against any outside elements generating harmful energy. The method I outlined earlier for protecting the house itself can be similarly utilised to guard the interior. Take the following typical situations as examples that are easy to adapt to any situation, and then refer to the table opposite for specific guidance.

- If your outside view is marred by such commonplace features as a lamp post or a telegraph pole—the element here is WOOD—it requires something made of METAL like an iron vase or copper bowl placed on the window sill to counter the harmful influence.
- A view of pointed roofs or a church spire is symbolic of FIRE and can be controlled by WATER—perhaps in the form of a pot plant standing in a well-watered bowl.
- A vista of rows of flat roofs representing EARTH should be opposed by WOOD in the shape of a wooden carving or small box made of wood.

OUTSIDE INFLUENCE	INDOOR CONTROL
FIRE (Pointed roofs, church spires)	WATER (Bowl of water, drinks dispenser)
WOOD (Poles, posts and trees)	METAL (Iron sculptures, white ornaments)
EARTH (Flat roofs, low buildings)	WOOD (Indoor plants, green decorations)
METAL (Iron structures, scaffolding)	FIRE (Red candles, incense holder)
WATER (Utility wires, pylons)	EARTH (Stone jars, yellow statues)

- If electrical installations, symbolic of WATER, are the problem, then place a suitable stone jar or piece of ceramic pottery representing EARTH in the window.
- Should the problem be an ugly gas-holder or iron bridge, symbolising METAL, its influence can be offset by FIRE in the form of some ornamental candles on the ledge.

One final point about windows. Their shape is important: square and rectangular windows will encourage the flow of *Chi*, while pointed windows are believed to be symbolic of fire and can tempt fate.

GOOD LUCK CHARMS

Charms and talismans have played a significant part in household Feng Shui for many centuries. Probably quite a few people will be familiar with the most popular of these tokens, for they are also common fixtures in Chinese restaurants and shops all over the world, hanging on walls, doors or in the windows.

A *ba-gua* good luck talisman.

Most of the charms are of great antiquity and utilise the pre-eminent symbols of Feng Shui, such as the Azure Dragon/ White Tiger configuration, the Yin and Yang symbol, and the influential Eight Trigrams. Frequently the trigrams are combined around the Yin and Yang symbol and carved onto an octagonal piece of wood, or else printed on cardboard and hung up for good luck. Indeed, I have come across examples of these *ba-gua*—as Feng Shui calls them—in homes all over the world from Melbourne to Singapore, and from San Francisco to Soho. They are also much in evidence in shop windows, and although often imagined by foreigners to be there purely for decoration, are actually highly functional in protecting the premises against bad *Sha*.

The *Luopan* compass is also a powerful charm against the *Sha* and I have seen them propped up on their sides in the corners of numerous rooms of Chinese homes in order to deflect the 'noxious odour' out of the building.

Ancient Chinese coins which are said to be symbolic of wealth and prosperity may similarly be seen affixed to the fronts of houses, as well as engravings of other luck-bringing symbols like birds, fruit and plants. Figures of animals are much in demand by the Chinese as charms—with lions and tigers almost equally matched in popularity by representations of dragons and dogs.

The tortoise and the goldfish have also had a special place on Feng Shui artefacts for centuries—the slow-moving creature being symbolic of longevity and the fish attracting good luck. Interestingly, in Chinese the word for fish sounds almost exactly like the word for success.

Feng Shui says that even the characters for such good luck charms can work just as well, and a *xiansheng* in Singapore presented me with the little table below of those which he said were most widely used on talismans. The reader is welcome to copy them for use in his or her own home!

祝	Bamboo	Good Luck
鹊	Bird	Extra Happiness
吉	Fruit	Luck
如	Fish	Success
寿	Old Man	Long Life

The characters for each of the Eight Trigrams are similarly said to harbour good luck when the sign appropriate to the member of a household is inscribed on a plain white background and then hung in his or her sleeping quarters. These are the respective characters for those who would like to enhance the *Chi* of their bedrooms:

Ch'ien 乾

Sun 巽

Li 離

Kên 艮

Tui 兌

K'an 坎

Chên 震

K'un 坤

Some of the household talismans are not illustrated at all, but carry inscriptions of time-honoured mottoes which are intended to encourage the flow of *Chi* through a building and drive off the baleful influence of *Sha*. 'Magic writing' is another part of this tradition and for many years the Chinese have inscribed secret formulae onto sheets of paper which are then sealed in envelopes and affixed to a beam or a wall in order to drive off evil spirits. The wording of these, however, tends to be the jealously guarded preserve of the professional geomancers and tailored to suit each individual client.

However, thanks to the kindness of the *xiansheng* in Singapore who helped me with much of the research for this book, I can illustrate two authentic Feng Shui charms here, one of which is intended for the home and the other for an individual. Number One is a charm that can be hung in a house where the rules of Feng Shui about orientation, the allocation of rooms, and so on, have been applied, and is intended to seal the happiness of its occupants. Number Two is a talisman to attract good fortune to its owner and help him or her secure wealth.

Number One   Number Two.
Two Good Luck Charms.

Some of the talismans may not be immediately obvious as such, because Feng Shui says that there is a number of everyday household items which can help in promoting happy living by deflecting evil influences—in particular crystal pendants, wind chimes, bell charms, gongs, fans, swords and, of course, mirrors. Even pot plants, candelabras, pottery and fans can help the *Chi* to circulate effectively when strategically placed.

Experts in Feng Shui are frequently asked how such basically mundane objects can be an effective barrier against bad *Sha*. Their answers are equally straightforward: a fan blows it away, a mirror reflects it back upon itself, and all evil spirits are weakened by iron objects such as swords.

When I pressed one of these *xiansheng* to say just how lucky he thought the various charms and talismans around his home had made him, he shrugged his shoulders, smiled enigmatically and replied, 'I do not know—but who knows how much *bad* fortune they have averted?'

In several Chinese shops I have also seen pairs of scissors hanging above the doorway, and one owner explained thàt they were there to 'cut' any bad luck before it entered the premises. This same man also pointed out to me the similarity between the Feng Shui cycle of destruction as outlined by the Five Elements and the famous 'Paper-Stone-Scissors' game which is so popular with children, both in China and the West.

In this game, as you may recall, the palm is a sheet of paper, the closed fist a stone and two fingers represent the scissors. After counting to three, each player indicates one of the shapes and a winner is decided. The order is: paper can wrap up a stone, so it is the winner; a stone is too hard for scissors to cut, so the stone triumphs; while as scissors can cut paper, the scissors come out on top.

My Chinese friend claimed that this game had actually evolved from Feng Shui centuries ago, and although I knew it was also of considerable antiquity in the West, I had no evidence on which to take issue with him.

In large Chinese communities like those in Singapore, Hong Kong and San Francisco, inexpensive booklets have long been available providing lists of hundreds of good luck items, as well as inscriptions, charms and spells to lift curses. Pictures and statues of Chinese dieties are frequently found in these publications and are said to function in rather the same way as gargoyles on Western churches. Among the most popular with Feng Shui adherents are the Buddha, a number of the Taoist saints and specific dieties such as Kiang-tse-ya, who is associated with the principles of *Yin* and *Yang*, and the God of Longevity whose presence is said to be beneficial to all the members of a household.

李老君

A popular Feng Shui illustration of a venerable Taoist
with the *Yin* and *Yang* symbol.

Inscriptions on lucky charms can be many and varied, but wholly dedicated to preserving the owner and warding off the evil influence of *Sha*. They are usually written in red ink on (ideally) a peachwood board about a foot long. A motto found on talismans both inside and outside many Chinese homes reads, *T'ai Shan Kan Tang*, which translates as 'This Stone, from Mount Tai, is Worthy'. Mount Tai is a famous sacred mountain in China, and for many years stones cut from it were set into the walls of buildings for protection against evil influences.

These 'lucky' stones were most often seen in Chinese towns in the wall of a building located exactly opposite the end of a street which opened into, but did not cross, the street on which the building stood. The belief was that they would cause any lines of Sha coming down the street to turn at right angles from the building and not enter it. Today these stones have largely been replaced by small wooden placards or banners, but still carry the same words seeking the protection of the sacred mountain.

Good fortune is also intended to be attracted by the ingenious method of preparing a piece of red paper on which are written four Chinese characters which translate as 'May he opposite me receive happiness' or 'May he opposite me secure wealth'. These are then fixed to a wall opposite the door of the person who is seeking to benefit. As the word 'me' in either of the sentences refers to the slip of paper, it will be seen at once to apply to the man across the road who stuck it up!

風 水

4 *ROOMS FOR IMPROVEMENT*

A home, whether it is a large house or a small flat, is of course
the sum total of its individual parts, and Feng Shui has specific
guidelines for each room in order that a harmonious environment can be achieved throughout. These rules have evolved
from the basic ideas devised by the first Chinese exponents, and
although their homes were rather different from those of today,
the principles they established have proved timeless. I propose
to give you a few pointers about rooms in general before
discussing each one individually.

One of the single most important elements is that all rooms
should be square, or at least rectangular in shape. This is
because the ancient sages believed that the square was symbolic of the earth and therefore balanced geometrically. Hence
even a single-room flat that meets this requirement immediately stands a better chance of enjoying good Feng Shui.

Irregularly shaped rooms are said to contain 'Dead Areas' in
which the *Chi* can be prevented from circulating and therefore
becomes stagnant. Where such corners exist, they should be
filled by the positioning of a substantial piece of furniture such
as a clothes cupboard, chest of drawers or display cabinet in
order to 'regularise' the shape.

According to one of several little Feng Shui chapbooks I

purchased in Singapore (complete with the most curious illustrations, one of which is reproduced here) the *Chi* is also better able to circulate in rooms of specific geomantic dimensions. The *good* dimensions are between:

Feng Shui offers guidelines on ideal room sizes.

- 0 to 5.375 centimetres.
- 16.125 to 26.875 centimetres.
- 37.625 to 48.375 centimetres.
- Plus any multiple of 43 centimetres added to the above.

The *bad* dimensions are:

- 5.375 to 16.125 centimetres.
- 26.875 to 37.625 centimetres.
- Plus any multiple of 43 centimetres added to the above.

Evidently, these figures have been accepted for centuries and were originally devised by the first *xiansheng* from a study of the Eight Trigrams and the *I Ching*, although precisely how these wise men reached such specific figures still remains a closely guarded secret.

However, to remedy any room which is considered to have bad dimensions, I am assured that if you add bookshelves or similar wall fixtures to reduce the dimensions, you will solve the problem.

Sloping ceilings are considered bad Feng Shui because they can impede the flow of the *Chi*. Those lovely oak beams and wooden rafters that are frequently found in old British houses are said to oppress the *Chi*, and it is courting trouble for anyone to sit in a chair or position a bed directly underneath them. The baleful influence of any such beam can, however, be mitigated by hanging a good luck charm such as a chime from it to channel the breath of life past it.

Rooms with solid walls have always been more favoured by the Chinese than those with partition walls. The primary reason for this is that the solid wall is said to be symbolic of security and the 'Azure Dragon/White Tiger' alliance of mountains. It is also claimed to be a throwback to the early days of Chinese civilisation, when many a home had to be fortified against the unexpected attacks of enemies or evil spirits. Not unreasonably, the protection of a solid wall was believed to be able to withstand such depredations for longer than a hollow one.

For the same reason, Feng Shui recommends placing chairs and sofas that are regularly used with their backs to solid walls rather than partitions. Ideally, these seats will enable those sitting in them to look out of a window with a pleasant view.

Partitions do, however, have a part to play in Feng Shui, because the ancient art says that as the number of occupants of a home increases or their needs change, then the house should be versatile enough to allow changes to be made. Alterations to the structure of the average house or flat may well not be possible, or even feasible, but to have partitions that can be moved or fittings that can be dismantled and re-erected elsewhere is strongly recommended.

The sudden appearance of an unfavourable element outside a property—such as new buildings or poles belonging to one of the utility services—may well require internal changes that have to be augmented by subtle movements to the layout. Even if the *Chi* is not affected by such developments, the arrival of children may well require some rearrangement which the shifting of partitions can achieve without influencing the home's Feng Shui.

The lighting and colour scheme of a home are also important in establishing a harmonious environment in which people can be comfortable and relaxed. If proper care is *not* taken, then the adverse climate will surely affect the health of the occupants, and, in turn, their creativity and prosperity.

Feng Shui says that ideally a home should be lit by daylight and artificial lighting in equal degrees—just like the balance of *Yin* and *Yang*. Too much glare from outside can be as bad as harsh lighting inside.

Where glare is a problem—usually in towns and cities where the sky is seen against the dark background of other buildings—then blinds or net curtains have been the Chinese remedy for many centuries and can just as easily serve in a modern Western home. In some cases, an awning over the window may prove even more effective. Do not, however, diffuse the glare at the expense of ventilation, for the smooth flow of air also aids the *Chi*.

In built-up areas it is all too easy for the interior of properties to become hard (*Yang*) through over-illumination when softer (or *Yin*) lighting would better serve the residents. Light and colour also influence the warmth (*Yang*) or coldness (*Yin*) of the premises.

All colours are either *Yin* or *Yang*, and are divided like this:

YIN	YANG
Green	Red
Blue	Yellow
Purple-Blue	Purple-Red
Grey	Orange

The balance between these colours is achieved by ensuring that they are of equal strength—avoiding, for example, a fire engine red with a pastel green. It is also important to make sure that, if strong colours are used, they do not create a contrast that is uncomfortable to the eyes.

Another little Feng Shui booklet in my possession offers some interesting advice on the colour schemes for use in a study or workroom where it is important to enhance creativity. Because of its particular interest for those of you who work from home, I thought it worth including here.

The list is based on the reader's horoscope, and as the Chinese have a cyclical calendar of years named after twelve animal signs, the reader will first need to establish under which sign he or she was born. (For your guidance, the year in which the present book was published, 1993, was the 'Year of the Rooster' which began on January 23.)

SIGN	COLOURS
Rooster	White, red and yellow
Dog	Yellow, white and red
Boar	Yellow, white and red
Rat	White, red and green
Ox	Yellow, white and red
Tiger	Yellow, white and red
Rabbit	White, red and purple
Dragon	White, green and red
Snake	White, green and red
Horse	White, green and red
Sheep	White, green and yellow
Monkey	White, green and yellow

It is certainly true, from my own experience, that the Feng Shui of many a dark and gloomy home has been vastly improved by the introduction of the right colour scheme, especially where it matches the owner's natal sign. Equally, where there is little natural light, this can be enhanced by the introduction of a few strategically placed lights—if possible with diffuser switches. Even the ancient Chinese knew how to control the lighting in their homes by raising or lowering the wicks of their oil lamps.

When it comes to the actual decoration of rooms, Feng Shui stresses that the colours should suit the requirements whether they are for working, relaxing, dining or sleeping. It is essential to establish a sense of balance between these colours and the furnishings—the *Yin* and *Yang* forces yet again—and never to allow the space to become cluttered with too much furniture, since this will disrupt the flow of *Chi*. The more tranquil the setting, the more effective the energy force will be in revitalising the occupants.

The colour schemes favoured by the Chinese for their homes date back to the days of the first Imperial households when they were established according to Feng Shui principles. Red was a widely used colour because of its association with happiness and prosperity. Yellow was also popular with the ruling families because it symbolised authority and gaiety, while green was the favourite with the people because it promised peace and long life. Blue symbolised blessings from heaven and white stood for purity.

Gold has been popular in China for many centuries and is frequently used in conjunction with red to mix good luck with wealth. In fact, experts often advise painting any rooms that have very poor outlooks with strong colours such as red and gold; while small, oppressive rooms are best in light, pastel shades. Any room with a poor aspect would benefit from a black door, it is said, though this should not face south for, as we saw in Chapter 2, page 38, black is the colour of the ill-favoured north. Equally, it is bad Feng Shui to paint a door or wall facing west in red.

Paintings can also be beneficial to a room, especially if hung in matching-sized pairs and featuring picturesque landscapes, plants or animals; while wallpaper, curtains and carpets will help the overall ambience if they feature patterns with symbolic associations such as trees (long life), clouds (heavenly blessings) and water (wealth). Further examples of this, as well as the use of fish tanks, plants and animal sculptures, will be discussed in the appropriate room sections that follow.

THE DINING-ROOM

As the dining-room is an important area of the home where the family gather together or where those living on their own entertain friends and relatives, it has always had a special place in Chinese life. According to Feng Shui, the best position for this room is at one of the corners of a property, ideally on the southern side, with windows looking either eastwards or westwards. This will particularly stimulate the *Chi*, which some experts believe can centre on the dining-room in some homes. Where the windows of your home do not meet this requirement and there is a threat to the room's Feng Shui from an outside element, then you should turn back to page 69 where suggested countermeasures are listed.

The dining-table, as the centre-piece of the room, should be placed so that guests can walk round it to their places without bumping into other furnishings. The ideal table is round, being symbolic of heavenly blessings, and considered by Feng Shui tō be superior to the square or oblong table which signifies the earth and is therefore inferior.

The rectangular table much favoured in the West will not damage the Feng Shui so long as those who sit round it adhere to the positions decreed for the family by the Eight Trigrams, as explained on page 66. There we were discussing the allocating of sleeping quarters, but around the dining-table the order is similar as this diagram will help explain:

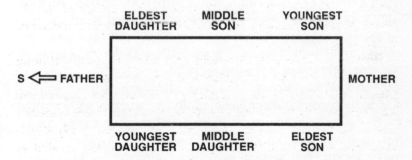

Just as the English have a superstition about 13 being an unlucky number to place around a table, so the Chinese believe that the number of seats should always be an even one. Chairs with good backrests not only provide a comfortable position for the diners, but protect their exposed backs in the time-honoured manner against a sudden attack. Seats with arm rests in the horseshoe shape of the 'Azure Dragon/White Tiger' configuration are naturally recommended by Feng Shui.

The most favoured colour schemes for a dining-room are either yellow (representing gaiety) or green (for contentment), and it is important to make sure that there is an even light illuminating the dining table. Mirrors are a good thing to have hanging on facing dining-room walls, for they add to a feeling of spaciousness in the room.

THE KITCHEN

Both the direction in which a kitchen faces and the positioning of the various pieces of equipment in it are important, according to Feng Shui, for it is in this room that the elements of Fire and Water come into close proximity and can all too easily give a sinister meaning to that old Western saying, 'More accidents happen in the kitchen than anywhere else!'

Appropriately, the Chinese character which results from the Fire element being joined with that of Water translates as 'disaster'.

As I explained earlier, the Chinese regard the north with apprehension because of the devils that are supposed to dwell there and also as it is the direction from which bad weather comes. Hence a kitchen facing north is exposed to all the evil forces. In Feng Shui the obvious measures to this situation are either a small wall (*Ying Pei*) opposite the back door, or counter-elements on the kitchen window sill.

Even more important is the layout inside the kitchen which, if it is not propitious, can, hopefully, be altered without too much difficulty or expense. The crucial point to remember is not to have items of equipment which are symbolised by opposing elements next to each other, thereby increasing the risks of danger.

The cooker (FIRE) should ideally be situated on a wall facing south or east, and as far away as possible from the refrigerator or sink (WATER). On no account place the cooker in a corner where there is poor lighting or bad ventilation, for this will encourage the forces of *Sha* to cluster. Feng Shui recommends that the ideal position for a sink is beneath a window with a good view.

If it proves impossible, or impracticable, to avoid the cooker and sink and/or refrigerator being adjacent to one another, then Feng Shui insists they should be separated by shelves or cupboards containing utensils such as china plates and copper pans which represent the counter-elements of EARTH and METAL. These will provide a 'barrier' between the potentially dangerous elements.

A word of warning about where cutlery is stored. Feng Shui says that knives, forks, spoons and all the other implements for eating and preparing food—which are represented by the Metal element—should not be kept in a 'dead' area where the *Sha* influences can gather and put the residents at risk of 'cutting' their health. All work surfaces should be well lit, too, with white, the colour of purity, being an ideal kitchen décor.

Finally, it is not good Feng Shui for the kitchen to be next door to a lavatory, for this can pollute the *Chi* before it enters the room. Fortunately, this rarely seems to occur in Western homes.

THE LIVING-ROOM

Like the kitchen, the least auspicious direction for a living-room to face is towards the north. The Chinese have always believed that as the living-room is mostly in use in the late afternoon and evening, one facing west has a special appeal. Ideally, too, it should look out over a garden or some other scenic view. Where these conditions cannot be met, or the outside elements are hostile, then the reader will once again need to refer to page 69 to determine which counter-elements must be utilised to improve the Feng Shui.

A good situation for the living-room in any single-storey building, apartment or flat is next door to the bedroom—so allowing the *Chi* to flow through them both—while in a home that has two floors it should be directly below the bedroom, which will allow the breath of life to pass through it after it has circulated up the stairs.

Bearing in mind how the influences of *Chi* and *Sha* move through a house, and the fact that people spend an appreciable part of each day in the living-room, the shape is also important. Square, rectangular and generally neatly shaped rooms allow the *Chi* to waft easily, while irregular shapes have the opposite effect. Of all these, the square-shaped room is said to be the most auspicious because it symbolises the security of the earth.

If the shape of the living-room is not conducive to generating an atmosphere of domestic peace and contentment, then good Feng Shui can be achieved by erecting a partition to cut off the offending area, thereby transforming it into a regular shape. A screen with a dragon pattern such as the one below is said to be particularly effective:

The ceiling of the living-room should also be taken into consideration. A sloping ceiling does not permit the smooth flow of the *Chi*, and exposed beams are also said to be unlucky. If the ceiling cannot be changed or the beams covered, then a talisman such as the chimes or a symbol of the Eight Trigrams should be suspended from either to counter the development of any *Sha*.

Care should be taken, too, with the arrangement of furniture. In Feng Shui, no chair should have its back to a door or window—although they can be positioned at right angles to these features. A Chinese belief dating back to the earliest times stresses that the seat usually occupied by the head of the household should especially not have its back to either a door or a window because this would enable enemies to creep up on the person without being seen. Today, it might be said that it is more likely to lead to them developing rheumatism or a cold! If possible, this seat should always face the favoured direction of the south—although never directly facing a window because the glare, which is *Sha*, can adversely affect the occupant. For the same reason a television set should never be placed in front of a window, as this makes it difficult to view.

If the living-room is propitiously situated next door to the bedroom, do not ruin the Feng Shui by arranging the seats in such a way that they form an arrow-head shape (↑) pointing at the sleeping quarters. Symbolically, this is a threat to those who sleep in the bedroom—and all the more so if the bed is positioned so that its foot faces the door. The Manchester flat of an acquaintance of mine who had been sleeping badly and suffered a run of misfortune in her life was diagnosed as harbouring *Sha* because the bedroom and adjacent living-room were laid out in precisely this manner. The balance was restored by readjusting the furniture as shown overleaf.

The number of chairs in a living-room should always add up to an even number, and the Chinese have for centuries believed that the best seats are those shaped like tortoises, for they are symbolic of longevity.

Colour schemes in the living-room can vary according to taste and temperament. Feng Shui says that yellow or white are most appropriate in this room because of their associations with the ancient Chinese imperial households where they were decreed to be symbolic of authority and purity. The colour blue represents heavenly blessings, green longevity and red happiness, glory and luck. Mirrors are excellent fixtures because of their ability to deflect *Sha* should the need arise, while paintings of scenic landscapes combining the *Yin* and *Yang* balance of water and rocks acting in harmony are also most suitable. The Chinese often hang pictures and wall ornaments in pairs, acknowledging the importance of *Yin* and *Yang* and an even older belief that happiness comes in twos.

A fish tank in the living-room is likewise a symbol of good fortune. Feng Shui says that goldfish are particularly lucky creatures and can deflect the evil influences of *Sha* away from the occupants. Designs featuring goldfish have also been regarded for many centuries in China as symbols of success.

Although many of us in the West love fresh-cut flowers from the garden in our living-rooms, Feng Shui declares that plants such as cacti and bamboo, which grow in the harshest conditions and live for many years, are better luck bringers than blooms which invariably fade before long. Patterns based on

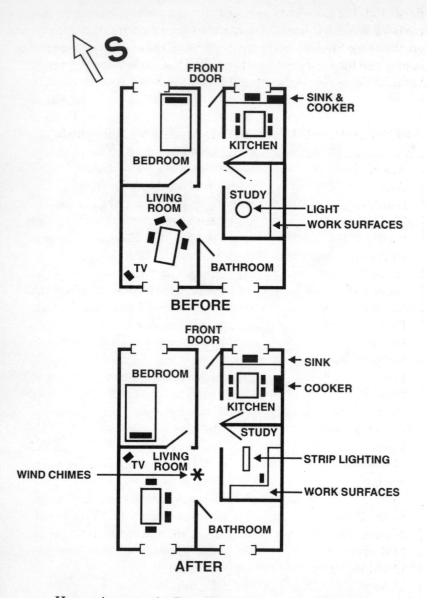

How to improve the Feng Shui of a typical small flat by rearranging the furniture and fittings.

flora and fauna which are utilised on wallpaper, carpets, curtains and furniture covers can also have an important effect on the Feng Shui of the room because of their special significance, and for your guidance here is an A-Z of the most popular Chinese designs and their good luck omens.

FENG SHUI PATTERNS AND THEIR SYMBOLISM

Acacia Tree	Permanence
Bats	Good Fortune
Bamboo	Long Life and Good Luck
Birds	Happiness
Chimera	Strength and Dignity
Chrysanthemum	Endurance and Long Life
Coins	Prosperity
Clouds	Heavenly Blessings
Cranes	Loyalty and Long Life
Deer	Good Luck and Wealth
Dragon	Strength and Authority
Elephant	Strength and Wisdom
Fish	Success and Plenty
Flowers	Wealth
Fruit	Good Fortune
Gold Objects	Wealth
Horse	Endurance
House	Unity and Good Fortune
Jasmine	Friendship
Lion	Strength and Majesty
Lotus Plant	Perseverance
Mountains	Strength and Endurance
Old Man	Longevity
Orchid	Patience
Orange	Wealth
Peach	Friendship
Pear	Long Life
Phoenix	Gracefulness and Wisdom
Pine Tree	Longevity

Plum Tree	Beauty and Youth
Pomegranate	Fertility
Rocks	Endurance
Rose	Beauty
Sky	Heavenly Blessings
Sun	Health and Happiness
Tiger	Strength and Stamina
Tortoiseshell	Longevity
Unicorn	Power and Position
Vase	Quietude
Water	Wealth and Heavenly Blessings
Willow	Gracefulness

THE STUDY

Typical Chinese houses tend to be one-or two-storeyed build-ings around a central courtyard, and any room adjoining this open space is believed to be suitable for use as a study. It is not essential that the room faces south, but ideally the window should be on the left-hand side and providing a pleasing view and an effective means of ventilation. If there is no window on the left-hand side, then by hanging a mirror on this wall which reflects the view from a window then the Feng Shui of the room will be satisfied. Take care, of course, to ensure that the mirror does not offend the code of the Five Elements by introducing an ill-omened factor from outside into the study.

Red is a popular colour for the study because of its associa-tion with auspiciousness and fame. Lighting is particularly important, too, for it must be purposefully directed and not allowed to cause a glare since this attracts the *Sha*. (In this context, spotlights are regarded as being good Feng Shui.)

Every study must have its desk, and this should be rectangu-lar in shape and placed against a solid, exterior wall. Chinese writers usually place small symbolic carvings on their desks, of creatures such as the dragon, which represents strength, and the tortoise, famed for its longevity. These models, along with such other powerful creatures as lions, tigers and elephants, are excellent protection against the *Sha*.

Plenty of space must be allowed for the books, documents and other materials which are usually found in any study—but Feng Shui suggests that there should be one small, uncluttered area where the occupier can withdraw from his work and give himself time for quiet contemplation. The Chinese call these spots *Ming Tan'g*, and the central feature is a single, high-backed chair—providing comfort for the occupant and 'protecting' his back against evil spirits. Behind it should hang a picture or talisman representing water. This is said to ensure the 'flow' of creative inspiration to the occupant of the study.

THE BATHROOM

Because Feng Shui states that the north side of a home is the one with the affinity to water, it is there that the bathroom should preferably be situated. It is also said to be important that this room should not adjoin the main entrance to the house or be adjacent to the kitchen, as it can thus 'pollute' the *Chi* even before it begins to circulate throughout the building.

If the lavatory *is* situated in either of these two locations, however, an effective 'barrier' must be erected, and as the bathroom is represented by the Water element which is controlled by Earth, then the use of ceramic tiles on the intervening wall will serve the Feng Shui. The fact that such tiles are often found in Western kitchens and lavatories is said to be another example of our unconscious use of the principles of this ancient art.

A separate lavatory is believed to be more beneficial than one in the bathroom, although it should be positioned against a wall convenient to a drain so that the polluted water is quickly disposed of. To ensure that there are no *Sha* influences emanating from the drain, it is important that it is covered, ideally with bricks or a tile.

Despite the popularity in the West for bedrooms with *en suite* bathrooms, Feng Shui says that this is not helpful to the house's good luck. According to the *xiansheng*, the reason for this is that in the bathroom the *Chi* which has been polluted must be replaced quickly before it can become *Sha*—and the last place anyone would want this to waft away to is into the bedroom where a pure and gentle flow of 'the breath of life' is essential. In Singapore, where many hotels have *en suite* bathrooms, I saw that Feng Shui had been complied with by curtains made of pottery beads, which separated one room from the other and discouraged the movement of *Sha*.

The colour blue, which symbolises heavenly blessings, is by far the most preferred colour for the bathroom, according to Feng Shui. Good *Chi* can be obtained, however, by decorating the bathroom with pictures that feature tall mountains and gently flowing rivers, such as the picture here of a bridge over the Papien River in China, which is to be found in many Hong Kong homes.

Pictures such as this are perfect examples of *Yin* and *Yang* co-existing in harmony. The water wheel is another popular motif. Perhaps, though, murals featuring fish are the most auspicious for any bathroom.

THE BEDROOM

It has been estimated that we spend at least one-third of our lives in bed and this, naturally, has led to the bedroom being given particular attention in Feng Shui. The bed itself, of course, is crucial and the position in which it should be placed in the room relative to the points of the compass is considered very important in order that the occupant can enjoy the benefits of the prevailing *Chi* and, in turn, experience restful and revitalising sleep.

The ancient sages who devised Feng Shui studied the heavens and determined that it was the movement of the planets that controlled every aspect of a person's life. They also reached four basic conclusions about the siting of the sleeping quarters within the layout of a home.

A directly north-facing bedroom, they felt, would be the least favourable orientation because it did not receive the Yang influences of the sun, while a south-facing bedroom had the disadvantage of being unable to maximise the *Chi* influence of the sun to the benefit of the occupants because it would not normally be occupied by day. They agreed that a bedroom facing west would probably be more suitable for adults and older people because it received the milder rays of the setting sun, whereas one orientated to the east would best serve the younger generation because it would receive the invigorating rays of the rising sun.

Having established these basic tenets, the *xiansheng* felt the need for more specifics, and turned their attention to the twelve points of the compass. Each of these, they decided, had a special relationship to the twelve years of the Chinese calendar. And just as a horoscope could influence a person's waking life, so the time he or she was asleep was similarly under the influence of one of twelve different directions—all dependent on the year in which the person was born. From their calculations emerged a table which offered guidance about the most suitable orientation for *anyone's* bed relative to their natal sign. To take advantage of the listing, all you have to do is check the orientation against your birth symbol (which you will no doubt already have worked out during my earlier discussion about the rooms of a home on page 81) and then use the *Luopan* or magnetic compass to make the alignment.

SYMBOL	ORIENTATION
Rooster	West
Dog	West-North-West
Boar	North-North-West
Rat	North
Ox	North-North-East
Tiger	East-North-East
Rabbit	East
Dragon	East-South-East
Snake	South-South-East
Horse	South
Sheep	South-South-West
Monkey	West-South-West

Where it proves impossible to align the bed precisely to the direction indicated, Feng Shui says that it can be placed in a geometrical direction not more than one degree either way. Therefore, if your sign is the Rooster and your direction West, you may face the head of your bed between South-South West to North-North West. Curious as this whole concept may seem to Western readers, it must be remembered that to Feng Shui skewing a bed—or a door or a wall—away from the danger of the 'Secret Arrows' of *Sha* is much more important than aesthetic appearance. Similarly, a bed does not have to be at right angles to the wall of the room in which it stands if there is a chance that this will inhibit the *Chi*. If you still find it imposs-ible to adhere to these guidelines, then you should seriously consider changing your sleeping area or picking another bed-room where the omens are more auspicious.

Feng Shui advises that no bed should face a window in a direct line as this will make it subject to glare which is, of course, bad *Sha*—as well as making sleep difficult. A good position is adjacent to a solid wall: this was regarded by the ancient Chinese as protecting the sleeper in the same way that a mountain protects a house in its lee. Conversely, though, a bed should never be placed parallel under a beam or beneath a sloping ceiling as this will make it vulnerable to the influences of *Sha*.

Although mirrors are considered an essential feature in most Western bedrooms, Feng Shui says that there should not be more than two of them as they will generate an over-abundance of *Chi*. Nor should any mirror be positioned directly facing the end of the bed. The reason for this is that the Chinese believe the human soul can leave the body while it is asleep, and seeing itself might give the spirit a shock and disturb the sleeper.

Any dressing-table that contains a mirror should not be positioned opposite a window because this will reflect the harmful glare of *Sha* all around the room. A mirror on the ceiling, however, is generally accepted to stimulate the flow of the *Chi*!

Another Feng Shui belief says that the foot of the bed should never directly face the bedroom door. The explanation for this is that in China the bodies of those who have died in bed are always carried out of the room feet first and then laid out with their feet facing the door of the mortuary. Hence sleeping in a bed facing the door is a bad omen.

Finally, bedrooms are better located on the upper level of a house or apartment, but in the case of flats or bed-sitters they are best sited adjacent to the central living area.

THE GARAGE

Although, obviously, the Chinese home of the past did not contain a garage, a workshop was by no means unusual and modern geomancers apply the old principles for them to their new counterpart. There are, in fact, many of the same perils to be found in the garage as there are in the kitchen—in particular a whole battery of sharp implements ranging from mechanical tools to gardening equipment, along with the proximity of the fire and water elements in things such as central heating boilers and deep freeze cabinets. So the rules I have already outlined about the positioning of such contrary items in the kitchen apply with equal importance in the workshop/garage.

Curiously, however, the ideal location for a garage is facing towards the north, because not being inhabited it does not require the light of the sun. A geomancer explained another reason to me: the north is represented by the symbol *K'an* in the Eight Trigrams, which is symbolic of circular motion—a factor present in many of the moving implements normally found in a garage. Another Chinese expert has also suggested that the explanation is much simpler: that the axle of the earth's rotation is found at the North Pole.

If there are exposed beams in the garage roof Feng Shui recommends that working surfaces or benches should run parallel to these and not across them. The ideal shape for a workshop or garage is square (because it symbolises the earth) and any door should open inwards to allow the *Chi* to enter.

風 水

5 HARMONY IN THE GARDEN

For centuries the garden has played a significant role in the
Feng Shui of Chinese homes. As we have already learned, the
early exponents of the art realised that the one way to counter
any elements which threatened a property was by putting up a
'protective' element close by, such as trees, a hedge or even a
small wall. As time passed, they also appreciated that they
could enhance their share of *Chi*—'the life blood of the living
earth' as it has sometimes been called—by introducing into
their gardens a variety of features such as paths, rockeries,
ponds, small pavilions and even plants and flowers of special
symbolic significance.

Indeed, the principle which had become obvious to the
xiansheng—that altering a room by changing a colour scheme,
realigning some furniture or introducing a mirror or lucky
talisman, could dramatically stimulate someone's well-
being—was actually very little different from a gardener
moving a plant closer to, or farther away from, the sunlight in
order to ensure its growth. Position and orientation were all-
important, and the old sages agreed that the *Chi* of a garden
could be made to work as effectively as it did in the house by
applying the same rules of Feng Shui about balance and
harmony.

A Feng Shui garden—an engraving from the *Yuan Ze* gardening manual.

According to one of the oldest Chinese gardening manuals, the *Yuan Ze*, a perfect garden is created when there are rough textures contrasting with smooth—that is, stationary rocks balanced by running water. Therefore the best site for a garden would be on the edge of a lake with a view of the mountains. Here the *Chi* would always be in harmony with man and nature.

Today these principles can be seen in practice in many beautiful Zen gardens in countries such as China, Japan, Hong Kong and Singapore. It is also possible, though, for them to be brought to bear in a Western garden—even a small roof garden, patio or windowbox, where such miniature gardens are the only option. In this way, each garden, whatever its size, can play an important role in helping to channel the beneficial 'breath of life' into a property, while at the same time keeping out the harmful *Sha*.

In the Feng Shui garden, just as in the home, we soon discover that the interaction of the 'Five Elements' is central to balance and harmony, especially when there are outside influences that threaten the *Chi*. In order to counter them you need to establish the orientation of the garden and then introduce a controlling element. Let us first recall the directions associated with each of the five elements:

WOOD: North-East, South-West
FIRE: East
EARTH: North, North-West
METAL: South, South-East
WATER: West

Next, we should perhaps remind ourselves of the appropriate controlling element for any threatening feature:

GARDEN ORIENTATION	
Threatening Element	Counter-Element
FIRE (Spires, towers)	WATER (Pond, fountain)
WOOD (Poles, trees)	METAL (Sculpture, frames)
EARTH (Mounds, huts)	WOOD (Plants, summer house)
METAL (Iron structures)	FIRE (Red flowers)
WATER (Wires, pylons)	EARTH (Garden ornaments)

Armed with this information, and having established the direction in which your garden faces so that you know the element associated with it, you should be able to counter any threatening element from outside. To illustrate what I mean, if there is a feature classified as METAL overlooking a garden that faces in a WOOD direction, then there is a danger of 'wasting away' and the counter-element WATER needs to be introduced. To put this into everyday terms: if there is something like a lamp post or electricity pylon (METAL) outside a North-East facing garden, this can harm the growth of plants and should be effectively controlled by the creation of a small ornamental pond (WATER) or by growing red flowers (FIRE).

It may happen, of course, that a garden facing either South or South-East is overlooked by these erections, but as the matching elements do not clash with one another no counter-measures are required. Only if the lamp post faces the front gate on a direct line to the front door—as I mentioned in Chapter 2—would a small bend in the path be necessary to enable the smooth flow of the *Chi* to the home and garden.

History tells us that Chinese gardens were being laid out according to the Feng Shui principles at least a thousand years before the birth of Christ. Their aim was simply to balance the *Yin* and *Yang* of the property and its surrounding landscape through matching what human hands had made to that of nature. Only by doing this was it believed that the owners of the garden would be able to live in harmony with the natural cosmology and man-made environment.

It seems probable that the first Western visitors to China actually gained their earliest insight into the practice of Feng Shui through seeing some of the graceful pagodas which then dotted the countryside—some of them on the lands of great estates, others in the gardens of the homes of civic officials, and the remainder on common land beside villages. Some of the pagodas were towering constructions, while others were little bigger than the height of an average man.

Two types of Feng Shui pagodas sketched in 1896.

These elegant-looking creations with their varying number of stories and pointed crowns provided a sharp contrast in the eyes of the foreigners to what they considered the 'meanness' of much of the rest of Chinese architecture. The larger pagodas, either poised on hillsides or beside watercourses, certainly reminded some visitors of church spires back at home, and prompted one missionary, the Reverend M. Yates, to enquire of his Chinese interpreter whether they were, in fact, temples or religious monuments. Later, he wrote in *The Chinese Recorder and Missionary Journal* of 1868:

> While in the Canton province we came across one of these pagodas standing to the north-east of a village, five stories high, looking, at a slight distance, exactly like the common type of brick erections which stud the country. But this, on near approach, proved to be made of wood, and on closer inspection betrayed that it was put together on thin, light boards attached to a framework in such a manner that the whole thing could be taken down and removed without much difficulty.
>
> My interpreter explained that it had been erected by the local villagers in the hope of improving their Feng Shui. If their crops were good in successive years, if no pestilence descended upon them, and if, above all, their people should live in harmony and prosperity, then the experiment in Feng Shui would be declared a success.

Although giant, artificial pagodas such as the one mentioned by the Reverend Mr Yates are a rare sight in China today, a rather smaller garden variety has become a standard ornament in many rural properties. They are nowadays made of porcelain and usually located at the foot of rockeries constructed to resemble miniature versions of the protective Azure Dragon/ White Tiger alliance. In the main they are placed in the Feng Shui-recommended south-west direction, although some Chinese favour a north-east orientation.

Much more widespread than the use of pagodas, however, has been the introduction of lines of trees or the building of walls to afford the home the protection of that traditional mountain range. Both are most commonly found where the landscape is flat, though they can be equally important where there is a lone hillock or small mountain representing an element that is threatening to the property.

Feng Shui says that trees planted for this specific purpose

should be evergreens and prolific growers—the yew is considered especially appropriate. It is important, too, that they are allowed to grow naturally and not be subjected to continual cutting or pruning. Such trees must always be at the rear of a property, for a grove of trees at the front would surely hamper the entrance of *Chi*. However, where a single tree is necessary as a controlling element at the front of the house, the pine is said to be the most suitable. Incidentally, the pine—like the willow and the cyprus—is believed by the Chinese to be symbolic of longevity, and all three are said to be auspicious for any garden.

Brick walls built to serve the same screening purpose are most effective if they have curved corners, for this not only assists the flow of the *Chi*, but is believed to attract wealth, too. A wall that also contains square openings (symbolic of earth) and round ones (representing heaven) will help balance the *Yin* and *Yang* throughout the whole area. It is important, too, to ensure that the wall is in proportion to the height and width of the house it encloses—ideally it should be no higher than the lower sill of the ground floor windows unless these are very low, when it should be waist height.

The average garden in Western countries is generally square or rectangular in shape but can be made more conducive to the flow of the *Chi* by introducing appropriate features to give a feeling of balance and continuity. This can be achieved by building low walls which are linked to rocks, trees and plants and also by introducing meandering paths.

Zigzag patterns which reflect the shapes of mountains and the natural courses of rivers are also said to be essential to good garden Feng Shui. A straight path through the garden disperses the *Chi* too quickly and should be replaced by one that curves and wanders. Nor is it beneficial to have a straight line of trees on either side of a drive, but rather than cut down the trees you can make modifications such as curved border edges to rectify this situation.

The early exponents of Feng Shui who took a particular interest in the garden laid down a number of rules relating to the orientation of its main features. Using the *Luopan* compass—you can use an ordinary magnetic compass—they established the following ideal positions for each feature:

PATHS: The main paths are best in the western part of the garden.

TREES: Should be planted in the east and south-eastern areas, except when required for screening.

STREAM: A stream should be directed eastwards to help the *Chi*.

POND: Any man-made pond or watercourse is best in the south or east.

ROCKERY: Ideally situated to the north of the pond and incorporating a small waterfall.

WORKSHOP or GARAGE: The north or north-east are the preferred locations, but never in the south.

When appropriately located, each feature is said to have a symbolic importance:

● Paths following meandering courses are symbolic of long life.

● Trees represent strength and protection.

● Streams are said to be symbolic of wealth.

● Ponds, especially those which are stocked with fish, represent success and integrity.

● Rockeries, because of the shapes in which they can be constructed and the elements they may contain, are believed to be symbolic of continuity.

In the ideal Feng Shui garden, the rockery and pond should be close to one another. According to the ancient art, the rockery represents hills which are the source of life because they provide man with his water. They are therefore regarded as *Yang*. The pond, being water, is a *Yin* feature and will provide the necessary harmony. Where there is no rockery, a pond should have a small central island on which is placed a suitable *Yang* element such as a miniature gazebo or pavilion.

It is important to remember that any man-made pond should have a natural shape and not be made square or rectangular. The banks, too, should be sloping and planted with appropriate flowers, the water lily being considered symbolic of uprightness and a harbinger of good luck. Any bridge crossing a pond or stream should have steps and, if possible, be winding so as to avoid harbouring bad *Sha*. A pond that contains a flourishing collection of goldfish is said to bring the whole garden good luck.

It is not good Feng Shui to plant a tree on any island in a pond, however, as this is symbolic of confinement and trouble—but you would need a very large pond for this even to be a possibility.

The Chinese garden pavilion—the equivalent of our Western summer house—is also said to have special significance depending on the number of sides it contains. While the square construction is symbolic of the stability of earth, five sides are linked to the benefits of the 'Five Elements'. Six-sided pavilions symbolise wealth while those with eight sides, like the 'Eight Trigrams', indicate prosperity.

If your house has no garden of its own, but has either a patio or a roof garden, you can still take advantage of Feng Shui through the use of patterns, statues, flowers and plants.

For centuries the Chinese have made pebble mosaics in their gardens and these are ideal for laying in confined spaces. Such mosaics, where the design emphasises alternation of shape and pattern, are perfectly in keeping with the principles of *Yin* and *Yang* and ideal for patios and roof gardens. Here, too, miniature mountains and rockeries can be built to act as protective elements, in the same manner as in a larger garden.

While it is clearly not possible to plant trees in such a confined space, the use of symbolic animals in their appropriate quarters will benefit the property's Feng Shui: dragons in the east, tigers in the west, cranes or herons in the south and tortoises to the north. Any garden, regardless of its size, can also take advantage of the symbolic values of certain animal statues to enhance its luck. Sculptures of lions, for example, represent power and authority; storks symbolise youth; tortoises represent longevity; while deer can bring wealth.

The exponents of Feng Shui in the garden have given a great deal of thought to the *Yin* and *Yang* elements of flowers and plants that can play a significant part in the harmony and balance of your garden. They believed that the appropriate choice of flowers in any particular setting—a garden bed, a rockery, a patio or even a window box—would enhance the *Chi* of the property.

The best plants are those that have profuse foliage, blooms or fruits and are long-lived. They are believed to be symbolic of prosperity and longevity and, ideally, should be grown close to the house. From the observations of the Chinese gardeners of old, the list below has been drawn up as a guide to matching plants in harmony through their *Yin* and *Yang* qualities, as well as grouping them in ways that enhance the symbolism—for example, mixing pelargoniums and hydrangeas allies determination with achievement; and forsythia and jasmine together promote vigour and friendship. The choices are almost endless.

Feng Shui says that if you grow those plants that represent the desirable elements in your life, you are more likely to achieve harmony between yourself and nature. For instance, from the table you will see that no garden should be without viburnum or begonias: both have separate male and female plants which blend *Yin* and *Yang* in a doubly auspicious combination.

Some followers of the ancient art believe that beautiful flowers can become one of the most visible and rewarding features in a Feng Shui home, enshrining as they do the principles of harmony while at the same time enhancing the flow of the vital 'breath of life'.

FENG SHUI FLOWERS

Plant	Symbolism	Yin/Yang
Acacia	Stability	Yang
Apricot	Fruitfulness	Yin
Aspidistra	Fortitude	Yang
Bamboo	Youth	Yang
Begonia		Yin and Yang
Buddleia	Profusion	Yin

Chaenomeles	Resolution	Yang
Cherry	Fruitfulness	Yang
China Asters	Fire	Yang
Camellia	Evergreen	Yang
Chrysanthemum	Resolution	Yang
Cypress	Nobility	Yang
Delphinium	Consolidation	Yang
Euonymus	Modesty	Yin
Forsythia	Vigour	Yang
Gardenia	Strength	Yang
Hibiscus	Profusion	Yin
Hydrangea	Achievement	Yang
Hypericum	Profusion	Yin
Incarvillea	Flamboyance	Yin
Jasmine	Friendship	Yin
Juniper	Tolerance	Yang
Kerria	Individualism	Yang
Lilies	Profusion	Yin
Magnolia	Fragrance	Yin
Nandina	Holiness	Yin
Narcissus	Rejuvenation	Yang
Nomocharis	Tranquillity	Yin
Orchid	Endurance	Yang
Osmanthus	Evergreen	Yang
Peach	Friendship	Yang
Pear	Longevity	Yin
Pelargonium	Determination	Yang
Peony	Wealth	Yang
Pine	Longevity	Yang
Plum	Youthfulness	Yang
Pomegranate	Fertility	Yin
Primula	Fire	Yang
Pyracantha	Vigour	Yang
Rhododendron	Delicacy	Yin
Rodgersia	Profusion	Yin
Rose	Beauty	Yin
Saxifraga	Heavenly	Yang
Sorbus	Achievement	Yang

Spiraea	Marriage	Yin
Syringa	Fragrance	Yin
Thuja	Longevity	Yang
Viburnum		Yin and Yang
Virginia Creeper	Tenacity	Yang
Water Lily	Fortitude	Yang
Weigela	Profusion	Yin
Willow	Grace	Yin
Wisteria	Beauty	Yin

One last point. Some Feng Shui experts believe that those who have to confine their gardening activities to a window box or a few plantpots are best advised to plant flowers of the colours that coincide with their natal sign. The list on page 81 identifies these. Happy gardening!

風 水
6 *LOOKING TO THE FUTURE*

Emperor Fu Hsi, the first ruler of China, who is credited with having discovered the Eight Trigrams on the shell of a tortoise basking on the banks of the River Luo, also observed something else very remarkable on the sacred creature's back. This was a magic square of nine numbers—each in the form of a series of dots—in which every row of figures, horizontal, diagonal and vertical, added up to the same figure: 15. The Emperor named the square after the place where he had found it: the *Lo Shu*.

Stories about this unique square can be traced back to some of the earliest Chinese writings, especially those dealing with the evolution of Feng Shui. In the *Book of the Prince of Huai Nan*, written in the second century BC, the writer notes that not only do the numbers always add up to 15, but each of the odd, or *Yin*, numbers also accords with a cardinal compass point, while those in between are all *Yang* numbers.

It was the Emperor who first established a link between the *Lo Shu*, the compass and the Eight Trigrams. In his view, because each of the numbers on the square—with the exception of 5—faced one of the compass directions, each one, like the Eight Trigrams, must be associated with a compass point. You can see this for yourself if you turn back to the diagram on page 65, which shows the trigrams' association with the compass.

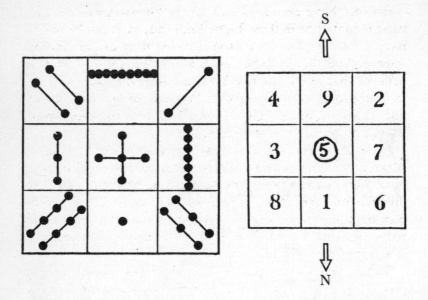

The magic square of nine numbers—the *Lo Shu*—observed by Emperor Fu Hsi on the shell of a tortoise. It is found in both versions shown here.

With this in mind it is possible to link each number with one of the trigrams, remembering that you should read the compass with the South at the top in traditional Chinese style:

    Number 9 = Li
    Number 2 = Ku'n
    Number 7 = Tui
    Number 6 = Ch'ien
    Number 1 = K'an
    Number 8 = Ken
    Number 3 = Chen
    Number 4 = Sun

From this list the Emperor was able not only to confirm an association between the numbers, directions and trigrams, but to use his findings as a way of pursuing the knowledge that we would all like to discover—what the future holds.

Because Feng Shui says that all the knowledge of the universe is contained in those Eight Trigrams, each can be said to have a message for the person directed to it by the ancient science. And thanks to the association with the *Lo Shu*, it is believed that by casting numbers and using the 'Rule of Nine' (a system also acknowledged in Western numerology) to reduce them to a single digit of 1,2,3,4,5,6,7 or 8, the appropriate trigram to consult can be determined.

For many centuries the Chinese used a bundle of 52 divining sticks, made from yarrow stalks between one and two feet long, in all these consultations. After being cast, the sticks were then divided and subdivided, thrown and thrown again, in a complex and time-consuming process, until it was at last possible to reduce the total by the 'Rule of Nine' to a single digit and refer it to one of the eight trigrams.

Today, you will be glad to hear, it is possible to achieve precisely the same result with just three coins, in a much easier and shorter ritual that has now been approved, practised and found successful by several generations of Feng Shui *xiansheng*.

First you must obtain three identical coins. These may be quite ordinary coins—so long as they have clearly distinguishable 'heads' and 'tails', as in the Chinese example on page 113 with a Dragon 'head' on one side and traditional characters on the reverse. If you cannot lay your hands on a suitable coin, since the purpose of this whole exercise is to find the 'value' of the trigrams, then you should use the side of the coin which shows its value as the 'head'.

Your aim when using the coins is to discover which of the eight trigrams fate intends you to be guided by. Before you begin, however, it is important to remember two things. Firstly, it is essential to be in a relaxed frame of mind and not to throw the coins with any thoughts of manipulating the result. Secondly, the three lines must be drawn on a piece of paper in the traditional Chinese fashion: starting from the *bottom* and putting one line above the other, allowing plenty of space between each line.

A Chinese coin of the type used in Feng Shui prophecies during the last one hundred years.

Now, taking the three coins and shaking them thoroughly in your cupped hand, throw them onto a flat surface. From the exposed faces it is possible to divine whether to draw a *Yang* or *Yin* line on your paper. A toss which produces two tails and one head is drawn as a solid (*Yang*) line, while two heads and one tail will mean a broken (*Yin*) line. Sometimes, of course, you may cast three heads, in which case the line should be written thus: 000, while three tails must be drawn as ↑ ↑ ↑.

According to Feng Shui, these lines made up from the same sides of all three coins are known as 'moving lines'. They can be used for options: either throw again for a completely new trigram, or else merely to change the line in question by a further throw. Over the years, exponents using the coin system have found the 'moving lines' particularly enlightening when casting the 64 hexagrams of the *I Ching*, as they provided them with more than one sign to consult—firstly, the hexagram created by merely changing the line in question; and, secondly, the 'second opinion' afforded by casting an entirely new hexagram. And how often do we find a second opinion invaluable in sorting out a problem!

Feng Shui has always stressed that the trigrams make up a system of philosophy based on the moral and mystical beliefs of the ancient Chinese, and it is wrong to expect to be provided with an actual 'positive' or 'negative' answer to any question. Indeed, it is essential for you to realise that you must draw on your own intuition to interpret the texts you are given—for they are, in truth, only intended as a guide to action. This holds true not only when using the eight trigrams for matters of prophecy and romance, but even more so in the greater variety offered by the 64 hexagrams.

As Raymond Van Over, a distinguished student of Chinese history and superstition, wrote in an introduction to an edited version of the *I Ching* published in 1970:

> It directs the questioner's attention to alternatives and the probable consequences of our actions if we choose one path instead of another. If the oracle wishes to direct our action in a specific direction or through a particular channel, it will tell us how a Superior Man would conduct himself. In this subtle way, our actions are directed towards a positive goal while still allowing us the free will to choose our own ultimate destiny.

Van Over and other writers like him have pointed out how important it is for those consulting this ancient system to have decided in their own minds what answers they are seeking *before* consulting the oracle. They should ask themselves such basic questions as *what* will happen if they carry out a particular action or project, *how* it will affect other people, and especially, which factors are likely to influence relationships with others, including members of the opposite sex. The answers are unlikely to be specific, but few vital questions such as these can ever be answered with a 'yes' or 'no'; however, no part of the text should be ignored or overlooked, for centuries of experience have shown that what at first might seem irrelevant can have a far deeper significance when thought about carefully.

The Chinese have always believed that those in authority should face south when giving an audience, so any book of questions should be on a table facing south which the questioner consults facing to the north. Burning incense is also considered conducive to a calm and responsive atmosphere.

Once you have thrown the three lines, you can then turn to the interpretations that have been produced for this book. These texts, I must stress, are merely the latest interpretations in a long line, for over the centuries something like 3,000 scholars have attempted to unravel the mysteries inherent in the simple, yet endlessly complex lines. What these men and woman have all agreed upon is that the lines are more valid than ordinary fortune-telling systems—certainly more complicated and venerable than the horoscope found in newspapers and magazines—because of the ideas and ideals which they embrace and their purpose of opening. up the questioning mind.

In a word, the more *intuition* you use when consulting the trigrams the greater the range of choice that will be open to you in deciding whether you are acting in accordance with your own best interests as well as those of your fellow human beings. As one regular consultant of the Feng Shui trigrams told me while we were discussing the powers of intuition—and the ridicule too often heaped upon them as a substitute for learning and knowledge—'Intuition is no more a supernatural gift than the ability to walk, run and jump, but like all of them its full development requires regular exercise.'

Feng Shui believes that because of the intimate relationship between heaven and earth and all they contain, nothing—the lives of people or the future—is unalterable, and that the structures of the trigrams have been provided as intuitive keys to what the future holds for us all.

PROPHECIES OF THE TRIGRAMS

On the following pages will be found texts giving interpretations for each of the Eight Trigrams, which you can refer to after throwing the coins and establishing which symbol you should consult. Each text gives guidance about future prospects, health and romance.

In some instances you will find the interpretations are remarkably specific and have, indeed, proved uncannily accurate during the many years in which they have been consulted—according to the Feng Shui *xiansheng* in Singapore who prepared them for me to pass on to a new generation of readers. The expert has also divided the answers into specific paragraphs to make for easier reading.

A typical Chinese fortune-teller.

1 CH'IEN
The Symbol of Creativity

Ch'ien *is a wholly male trigram consisting of three* Yang *lines and indicates that only the man who combines strength with gentleness will achieve true happiness. It symbolises the power of the celestial forces through which everything occurs. The superior man sets his eyes upon the example of heaven and strives to live up to its high ideals.*

GENERAL COMMENTS: *Ch'ien* represents the creative principle, *Yang*, which functions through change and ensures that everything is properly ordered: the sun shines, rain falls and men prosper. We must be subject to change and live in harmony with our environment. The lines of the trigram represent firmness, power and righteousness. The wise man knows he must use his strength of character to tackle his problems. We must all be like that man and be kind, well-behaved and merciful. There will be sadness soon, but friends will help you overcome this. Though you find yourself on the verge of a chasm (problem) there is no danger for you are not to blame. Because you have been vigilant you will obtain some material satisfaction. Although you are restless about the direction of your life, it would be wise to seek the guidance of a wise (older) person before taking irreversible decisions. This is an excellent time for reflection and contemplation about the future, without making any commitment.

FEMALE: Do not indulge in too much gossip for this is a threat to a potential love affair. A meeting with a man of position and influence could lead to marriage. Beware of flattery if you have not long left home, and do not attempt to cover your insecurity by arrogance. Always keep your views on love and marriage objective, for they may well give the wrong impression to someone who is potentially very important to you. If your social life seems restricted, take the opportunity to travel for this will lead to a new phase in romance. A sought-after pregnancy is now very likely.

MALE: A beautiful and apparently gentle woman is scheming to achieve power among a group of men at their expense. A meaningful relationship is being threatened by the intrusions of a third party. Flattery by women easily influences you, although you will soon enter into a lasting love affair in a most unexpected way. There is a danger of separation from someone you love through a misunderstanding.

BOTH SEXES: Emotions are the key to a successful love affair and they need to be carefully balanced between passion and affection. A marriage made now will not last for long.

2 SUN
The Symbol of Gentleness

Sun symbolises a gentle wind which spreads willing submission across the world. The superior man behaves always in accord with the rules of law. It is an auspicious sign for women and advises them to take full advantage of life and be prepared for surprises.

GENERAL COMMENTS: Although this trigram represents yielding to superior forces, it also encourages firmness in acting upon instructions to achieve success in small matters. It is important to have a goal in mind, although the success of this will be dependent on the gentleness of a great man (boss). Just as the wind varies in the direction it blows, so the wise man submits to circumstances he cannot control. Although you may be faced with a situation not of your own making, by refusing to act hastily you will resolve it. You are easily influenced, so beware of being used. We must not doubt our own intentions when dealing with friends. Do not allow your will-power to become exhausted because this will bring about shame. The wise man does not let a disorderly crowd affect his judgement, though they may blow him around like the wind. At work, inspire those beneath you to work in the company's interest and you will ensure your own good fortune. As a woman you can use gentleness to your own advantage, especially in expressing your opinions when they differ from those of your colleagues. The three days before and after an important change will be especially propitious.

FEMALE: This is a good time for romance and you may well find a new lover in the next six days. Do not persist in trying to revive an old love affair as this is already doomed to failure. By being prepared to alternate from submissive behaviour to persistence you will win your heart's desire. There is no harm in a sudden change of plan, especially if it involves travel with someone you secretly admire. An encounter that begins badly will work out well because of your happy nature and adaptability.

MALE: Do not play with the emotions of women at this time for it will rebound upon you. After a period of disagreements and quarrels you and the lady in your life will settle your differences and your love will be stronger than before. The older man who has been spending his time with a much younger woman will now become the subject of much gossip unless he has serious intentions of marrying her. Because of your versatility at taking on new tasks (promotion) you will soon meet a significant new girlfriend.

BOTH SEXES: Age should not be an issue in the affections of men and women, for love can conquer any such obstacles.

3 LI
The Symbol of Light

Li signifies a brilliant flame rising in two tongues which will illuminate and improve the world. The superior person will let his knowledge and influence shine widely and thereby ensure his own good fortune. It is an auspicious sign for couples whose love has blossomed through hardship.

GENERAL COMMENTS: A curious reference in the text for this trigram infers that aside from spreading your own influence, the rearing of cows will bring great success! The ancients believed this to mean that because the cow is a gentle creature needing careful attention to provide the best yield, the wise man should take care of all those less able than himself. The symbol urges us always to wear a demeanour of respect. Never take this sign lightly, for fire is no respecter of persons and you may well suffer a setback in your plans, especially if they have not been thought out clearly. Remember that after the brilliance of the sun comes the darkness of night and you should not waste your youth in idleness and dissipation. Sometimes strength is the answer to solving a dispute, but illuminate your argument by your knowledge rather than by threats. Do not weep, your troubles will not last. The imperial colour yellow is associated with this trigram and indicates a period of good fortune as long as, like a ruler, you are patient and listen to those who offer good advice.

FEMALE: You are an accommodating and caring woman and will not be fooled by false promises and flattery. It would be a mistake to become closely involved with someone from your own neighbourhood when there is the promise of a much more fulfilling romance away from home, perhaps even overseas. Do not dwell on the promises of someone who has been moved away by his work for he has already forgotten you. Your future happiness depends on hard work and co-operation with your lover.

MALE: Avoid being tempted by false pleasure and your relations with women will improve. An enduring love will blossom with someone you have known since childhood. A time of unhappiness will be followed by much joy through a sudden and unexpected meeting with a woman in a public place. You will be tempted by two beautiful women, one virtuous and the other immoral—but if you succumb to temptation all your good luck will disappear. Do not let your love of drinking threaten your romance.

BOTH SEXES: You are destined to have a happy family life, although you will not marry until you have achieved success in your career.

4 KEN
The Symbol of Meditation

Ken *symbolises huge, immovable mountains. The superior man knows the value of remaining still while contemplating his life and actions. This sign is a warning about exercising restraint at a time when things can easily go wrong; attention to small details will preserve a worthwhile relationship.*

GENERAL COMMENTS: The Chinese use the word 'stilling' to describe this symbol which represents the idea that the best form of action can be to refrain from action. It fits in with the West's concept of meditation and self-examination. This is a very strong personal trigram which recommends following your own inclinations about behaviour. The wise man says that if your inclination is to work, then work—but if you require rest, then take some rest! Only by being at one with your mind will you achieve peace and contentment. By ignoring the feelings of your heart you will let down some friends who have been counting on you. There is danger of an accident—but you will escape without injury, although the situation could have been avoided by closer co-operation with some of your friends. It is a good time for pursuing a long sought-after objective, though the answer to any particular problems relating to this goal will lie in clear thinking rather than in frantic activity. Distractions will surround you, but keep your reactions to yourself for emotionally you are in a vulnerable position.

FEMALE: This is not a good time for considering marriage or any permanent step in a relationship, for there are too many distractions around. Pride and arrogance resulting from a sudden business success can undermine your relationship to such an extent it will fall apart. Do not dress outrageously for although this will bring new men into your life, none will offer a worthwhile romance. Your real character is in danger of being swamped by the face you insist on showing to the world: you can be loved for yourself.

MALE: You will have to choose between two women in your life because three cannot live in harmony. Although you may soon have financial success, beware of dissipating this on a high-living woman for you will only be left with regrets. Do not try to conceal your sexual inexperience with idle boasting as this is also a hindrance to real romance. Everyone makes mistakes and to confess these to someone whom you admire will not end a romance, but strengthen it.

BOTH SEXES: The headlong pursuit of gratification is a very real threat to any meaningful relationship with a member of the opposite sex.

5 TUI
The Symbol of Happiness

Tui *symbolises a picturesque stretch of tranquil water representing the joys of happiness. The superior man spreads happiness among those he meets by praising all the virtues. The symbol suggests that the greatest achievements of men and women are together, although each must have his or her own identity and purpose in life.*

GENERAL COMMENTS: *Tui* promises that persistence in following the righteous course of heaven will be rewarded with great joy and success. The superior man knows that when the people are happy they forget their worries, tackle their problems with good heart and even forget they must die one day. Be careful about placing too much expectancy in a forthcoming event, though the disappointment will only be slight. You have been worrying unnecessarily about someone else's happiness at the cost of your own. The wise man knows that the greatest quality of happiness is in encouraging people, and your cheerful outlook is going to be a great asset at work in difficult times. Smile and the whole word smiles with you. Have confidence in your own ability and if you are unsettled look for a new job. Happiness does not come from chasing after superficial pleasures. You will not find joy by flattering other people, especially those with whom you are hoping to form a friendship. The superior person knows it is vain to pursue happiness because it resides within. Unexpected happiness is on the way!

FEMALE: If you are on the verge of becoming engaged or married there will be a delay, but one caused by good reasons and ultimately happily resolved. Beware of being selfish in your relationship and share both your pleasures and problems. You are not suited to sharing a home with another woman. Although you have to work with men whom you find boring do not ignore them for this will endanger your own position. A period of loneliness will be followed by one of your happiest romances.

MALE: There is no misfortune in putting yourself below a woman for the beautiful flower depends on the earth for its nourishment. It is not advisable to form a liaison with a woman much older than yourself for financial security. Do not use meaningless or flattering words to try and influence members of the opposite sex, for they will spread unpleasant gossip about you. Suspicions that the woman in your life is having an affair with someone else will prove groundless, so do not act hastily.

BOTH SEXES: Setbacks are part and parcel of any worthwhile relationship for they are the expressions of two different characters and will finally be united when the time is right.

6 K'AN
The Symbol of Obstacles

K'an *is symbolic of enormous watery depths. The superior man will need to be wary of the abyss into which he can fall without holding true to the virtues and encouraging others to avoid pitfalls. The sign also offers a warning against falling victim to lust for the implications can be long-lasting.*

GENERAL COMMENTS: Grave danger is signified by this trigram in which water represents a series of obstacles lying ahead. You will be faced with a number of problems in which you can easily drown unless you believe in your ability to succeed. There is no use in looking for short-term solutions nor taking a minor success as a signal that the danger is past. The river runs its course and the wise man must be steadfast and patient. This is an easy time to be misled, though the advice of someone in a senior position will be invaluable. You may run into deep waters, especially in a new relationship, and your course will be unclear until the intervention of a rock (true friend). Do little that will affect your stability. The help of certain relatives may be well-intentioned, but will not relieve the situation. Clear thinking of your own and an uncomplicated lifestyle are the best recipe for surviving the portents of *K'an*.

FEMALE: Do not behave in a disorderly or inconsiderate way towards the men in your life for they will soon avoid you. Seeking advancement and wealth will not endear you to members of the opposite sex. A rash love affair may be sexually satisfying, but will lead to unexpected complications with some of your oldest and dearest friends. Ignorance, whether real or feigned, is no excuse for taking risks with the lives and affections of others.

MALE: Beware of the woman who wants to spend money on pleasure without a thought for tomorrow; underneath her beauty she is immature and selfish. A romance is in danger because of a flirtation with a work colleague. Always listen carefully to the requests of women, but do not assume more than is spoken. This is not a good time to be contemplating marriage for your own life is too full of uncertainties to take on the responsibilities of a home. If you are careless in your affairs with women you will be forced to accept the responsibilities.

BOTH SEXES: Learn to behave with more maturity, for real love and romance await just around the corner.

7 CHEN
The Symbol of Disturbance

Chen symbolises thunder and movement and is immensely powerful. The superior man knows that although the terrible noise of thunder frightens people, it can also inspire them to change and improve themselves. The sign also suggests that patience is essential for the success of any relationship.

GENERAL COMMENTS: This trigram is said by the ancient sages to represent all the powerful natural forces of the earth which, by their awesome nature, can affect the minds of men. Fear is a good teacher, for by making us examine ourselves we can alter and find happiness. It is good not to let people see you are afraid when faced with confusion. For once, to act impetuously while you are frightened will not give rise to harm. Do not worry if you suffer a financial loss, for an opportunity to regain the money will soon present itself. Danger, in the form of evil people, will threaten social activities, but this will cause only apprehension and no real harm. You will have a premonition of troubles—warn others of this fact and by sharing your fears the dangers will be lessened. Fear of our neighbours makes us cautious. There will be much gossip about a marriage. A person who shares your innermost hopes and fears will soon come into your life—someone with whom you will have a lasting relationship.

FEMALE: There may be opposition to a marriage or partnership with a man whom your parents consider unsuitable because of class or financial instability. Take the advice of others rather than blindly opposing their wishes. Do not be proud or obstinate in your relationship with someone of whom you are fond, for this will only lead to unhappiness. Ostentation in clothes and manner will be a barrier to enduring friendships with members of the opposite sex. There is no harm in making a late marriage.

MALE: This symbol suggests that, if you have marriage in mind, be aware that the object of your affections will not make her mind up in a hurry. But by waiting patiently and courting her with love and consideration, she will agree and the marriage will be a happy one. Do not allow business matters to intrude into your love life for this will be detrimental to both. You are shy and modest and can get into the wrong company: beware of the attention of a promiscuous woman. To marry someone older than you may well be fortuitous.

BOTH SEXES: *Chen* cautions against rushing into an affair because there are many pitfalls lying in wait.

8 K'UN
The Symbol of Femininity

K'un is pure Yin *and symbolises the femininity of the terrestrial forces. The sign also represents the passiveness of Mother Earth from whom all things are born. This completely female symbol advises women to be virtuous and loving, for in this way they will fulfil their destiny.*

GENERAL COMMENTS: Though *K'un* is gentle and soft, it can still act with a tremendous power that engenders virtue. The symbol also represents development, healthy growth and energy for life. The ancient Chinese text calls this a very auspicious omen and suggests that those who accumulate good deeds will enjoy good fortune in abundance. It is wrong to boast of great talent or beauty because pride comes before a fall. Now is a good time to begin any public undertaking because, although it will not immediately succeed, the ultimate signs are good. Work with attention to detail and without haste, and remember it is not essential to be first or best. Following the example of others more senior or talented than you will bring success. It is an advantage to make friends in the south and west—people of a similar background and interests—but those to the north and east will be lost, for these are unsuitable people who will desert you when things go astray. *K'un* exemplifies glad acceptance which results in good fortune.

FEMALE: This is a good sign for a woman as it indicates that a current love affair will blossom. For the single girl, a new lover will come into her life in the next month. Use your own skills to augment those of the man in your life, for partnership brings the greatest good fortune and happiness. Do not make enemies of other women by spying upon them and gossiping about them for this will make you unpopular with men, too. Although you will be courted by two men, it will not be difficult to make a choice between them. Always ensure that your head rules your emotions.

MALE: Be confident in your dealings with women because they will come to understand your finer qualities. Good luck will result from a business meeting which involves a woman of importance, but do not be misled into thinking her interest is concerned with anything other than the deal. Your social life will improve dramatically, and a woman you previously met casually will now become much more important to you. Beware of an office romance for this points to bad luck.

BOTH SEXES: Through mutual respect and understanding a couple can expect the greatest good fortune in their lives together.

風 水
7 *THE WORLD OF FENG SHUI*

By one of those curious twists of fate, the practice of Feng Shui, which has been such a mainstay of the Chinese way of life for so many generations, is actually 'banned' by the present government in the People's Republic of China. But a tradition that has been a part of the nation's pysche for thousands of years is not so easily set aside and there is no doubt it still flourishes in the hearts of most of the big cities as well as in the vast rural tracts beyond, probably with the covert approval of many local party officials.

The decree outlawing the art as being a 'superstitious remnant' of China's imperial past and an affront to the Marxist faith in 'scientific atheism' was issued by the Communist Party after the Cultural Revolution in the Sixties. However, obedient to their leadership though the Chinese people are, the principles were too firmly established and tested by experience to be abandoned, and although Feng Shui certainly became less obviously evident on mainland China, it has spread instead to the rest of the world, carried by the refugees who fled from the Revolution as well as by those exponents already living in Chinese communities abroad who began proselytising its values. From Peking via Hong Kong, Singapore, Sydney, Los Angeles, San Francisco, New York and London, the message was soon spreading to the rest of the world—Feng Shui offered a new approach to living.

At first glance, the use of Feng Shui for attracting good luck might be put down as the popular explanation for its spread. Many of its followers, however, believe a deeper reason is the gradual rebirth of a universal acceptance of an ecological science which allies the best interests of the earth with all its life-forms, man included. These believers say that the aim of Feng Shui, quite simply, is to harmonise human interests with those of the environment, trying to ensure that each locality reflects as best it can the image of the earth as a natural paradise.

Apart from all those men and women around the world who have introduced the principles of Feng Shui into their private lives, there are also several very public signs of its spread in the shape of commercial buildings which have been built using its principles. I have had an opportunity of seeing several of these during my travels researching this book.

In China itself the greatest single symbol of Feng Shui is the fabulous Forbidden City in Peking, facing south across the now notorious Tienanmen Square, and considered one of the most splendid imperial residences to have survived the ravages of time and history. No visit to the country would, indeed, be complete without a view of this place of great riches and pomp which was for generations the palace of the nation's emperors. However, its connections with Feng Shui may not at first be apparent, although they have everything to do with the founding of Peking.

According to legend, Peking did not grow haphazardly like most of the world's great cities: every one of its palaces, residences, streets and gates was placed in accordance with a diagram based on Feng Shui principles which were revealed to the Emperor Yung Lo (1402–1424). The Emperor, nicknamed the 'Black Dragon', was the fourth son of the founder of the Ming Dynasty, Hung Wu. A forceful, cruel but brilliant man, Yung Lo was created Prince of Yen (Peking) and exiled from the then capital of Nanking because of the jealousy of the Empress.

The legend has it that before the 'Black Dragon' left the imperial court he was given a sealed packet by an old priest with instructions to open it only when he needed help or advice. When he finally arrived at what remained of the old city of Peking, which had been destroyed during the overthrow of the Mongol dynasty in 1368, he decided to open his mysterious parcel. To his amazement, he found inside a map of the future city of Peking, complete down to the last details, with instructions on how it must be built.

The new city was to be laid out in exact correspondence with a human body—that of a man named No Cha. The name was of course familiar to the Prince of Yen, for he had been a giant immortal of supernatural strength and prowess, about whom many legends had been told. What Yung Lo had to do was create a square, walled city which would represent his body, complete with head, heart, lungs, stomach and so on. The placement of the city, the inter-relationship of its component parts, even the furnishing of its chambers, were to be in line with Feng Shui principles.

Most Western readers are probably familiar with the appearance of the Forbidden City from the many photographs of it that have appeared in the press and hopefully can relate its shape to the Feng Shui map reproduced here, from which Yung Lo created his masterpiece of design and grandeur. The key to the various 'organs' of the 'body' and their relationship to the 'Five Elements' should be immediately apparent to those of you who recall the explanations given in Chapters 1 and 2.

Among the symbolic points which today's visitor can still spot easily are the three main gates in the south wall of the city which represent No Cha's head and shoulders; Pei Hai, to the west, is his stomach, and the north gate the end of his spine. Just looking at these features it is perhaps not too hard to understand the belief of generations of Chinese that Peking was an immortal city embodying the most basic tenet of Feng Shui in uniting a man with his dwelling. Small wonder, then, that when a new gate was cut in the wall of Peking in 1900, there were many who felt the Feng Shui of the city had been seriously damaged.

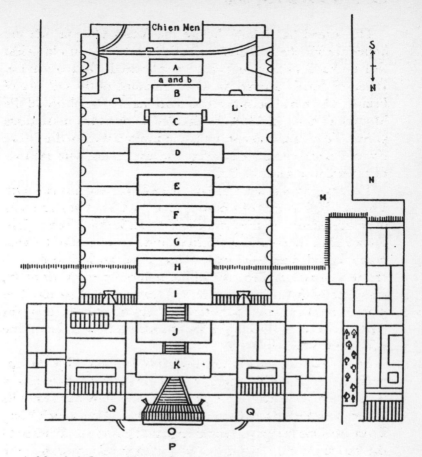

A Mouth, influenced by earth and water elements.

a & b Lungs, influenced by the element metal.

B & C The pericardium, under the influence of fire.

D The heart, under the influence of fire.

E Peritoneum, influenced by the element fire.

F A duct (said to connect the heart and liver) under the element wood.

G Liver, under the influence of the element wood.

H The gall, influenced by wood.

I An anatomical point between the kidneys (said to be a danger spot).

J The left kidney, under the element water.

K The right kidney, under the element fire.

L The spleen, under the element earth.

M The stomach, under the element earth.

N The navel, under the element earth.

O The end of the spine, under the element metal.

P The membrum virile, under the influence of water.

Q Large and small gutters. The large gutter comes under the element metal, and the small one under the influence of water.

Since then, however, further gates have been cut in the wall, a number of tall buildings have been erected which overlook the Forbidden City, and the San Tso Men, two wide stone gates with triple arches and curved roofs, that used to flank the east and west of the palace and were believed to be No Cha's lungs, have been destroyed. If the balance and harmony of nature has not been irreparably ruined by these losses, the people say, then the Feng Shui of Peking can surely survive any of man's depredations.

If the Chinese leadership of recent years has been showing scant regard for its Feng Shui traditions, the story elsewhere is quite different. In the enclave of Hong Kong, for instance, the authorities have for years co-operated with the builders of

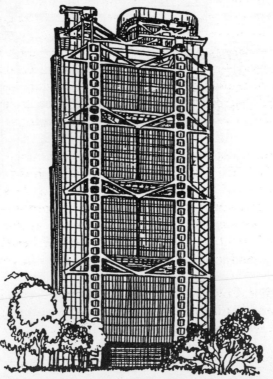

Architect's sketch of the ultra-modern Hongkong and Shanghai Bank in Hong Kong, which was built according to ancient Feng Shui principles.

many new business blocks, hotels and restaurants to allow them to adhere to the principles of Feng Shui. The luxurious Mandarin Hotel, for instance, conforms rigidly to the orientation rules, from its imposing entrance hall to the smallest rear door.

Probably the most striking example of Feng Shui in the colony is the 47-storey Hongkong and Shanghai Bank, situated at the foot of Victoria Peak facing the sea. The world's first billion-dollar structure, it was designed by the British architect, Sir Norman Foster, whose plans were shown to an expert in Feng Shui before construction began and some subtle changes suggested. Although the building has a hill at the back resembling the Azure Dragon/White Tiger alliance to protect it from evil influences and a view in front to enhance its 'intake' of wealth, there were immediate problems with the alignment of the escalators inside. Their direction had to be changed so that the 'up' escalators from the front entrance would encourage money to flow into the bank, while the 'down' escalators were positioned to stop it flowing out. Two bronze lions which had guarded the front of the old bank building were also moved to positions of honour outside the new superstructure to ensure its good luck.

An interesting story is also told about Government House, the white Colonial mansion which sits in the heart of Hong Kong. Because of its imposing, elevated position, the sweeping drive which leads up to the front door, and the cordon of trees to the rear, many local people were convinced that the original designer and architect must have been experts in Feng Shui, for the building and location satisfied every one of its conditions perfectly.

At the time Government House was being built, in 1874, there was another intriguing story current about Feng Shui in the colony, which was related by F. S. Turner.

The most malicious influence under which Hong Kong suffers is caused by that curious rock on the edge of the hill near Wanchai. It is distinctly seen from Queen's Road East, and foreigners generally see in it Cain and Abel—

Cain slaying his brother. The Chinese, though, take the rock to represent a female figure, which they call the bad woman, and they firmly and seriously believe that all the immorality of Hong Kong, all the recklessness and vice of Taipingshan, are caused by that wicked rock.

So firmly is this belief impressed upon the lowest classes in Hong Kong that those who profit from immoral practices actually go and worship that rock, spreading out offerings and burning incense at its foot. None dares to injure it, and I have been told by many otherwise sensible people, that several stone-cutters who attempted to quarry at the base of that rock died a sudden death immediately after the attempt.

In July 1997 Hong Kong is due to be handed back to the Chinese Government when the British mandate expires. The followers of Feng Shui in the colony are naturally waiting with some interest to see if the new rulers will attempt to quash the belief there, too.

Singapore is another place where Feng Shui flourishes. There are numerous hotels, high-rise apartments and especially restaurants which have been designed in accordance with its principles. I found an excellent example in the Novotel Orchid Inn on Dunearn Road, where I stayed during my visit. The hotel's restaurant, Dragon City, had been created with a tilted front door to capture good *Chi*, several talismans and ornaments to deflect the baleful *Sha*, and decorated in red, the colour of good luck and happiness. It was certainly a most harmonious environment and the food was excellent, too.

The Hyatt Hotel in the city was, apparently, rather unsuccessful when it first opened, until a Feng Shui expert spotted that the main doors faced north-west—which allowed evil spirits to enter—and the cashier's desk was parallel to the main road, which meant that money could flow out of the building rather too easily. With an adjustment to the doors and the building of two fountains to deflect the bad *Sha*, things quickly picked up.

For those with a taste for history, one of the best examples of

Feng Shui is the picturesque Guan Yin Tang Temple, built in 1886 on Telok Blangah Drive. It is situated on high ground, surrounded by small hills at the sides and rear, and faces dramatically out over the sea. It is said to have been modelled on the imposing five-storey Sea Guard Tower in Shanghai, another famous example of the principles of the ancient art in practice on mainland China.

When my travels took me on to Australia I once again found signs of Feng Shui among the Chinese communities. In

The famous Sea Guard Tower at Shanghai created by Feng Shui guidelines.

Melbourne's Chinatown, for instance, in front of shops in Little Bourke Street, there was evidence of the art being used in the shape of talismans adorned with the *Yin* and *Yang* symbols to drive away harmful influences; while in Victoria, at Bendigo which became famous during the Gold Rush, a number of Chinese emigrants built little houses utilising the art's principles, which still survive today and continue serving as happy homes.

According to experts, the Sydney Opera House represents Australia's most perfect example of Feng Shui. Its unique outline and prominent use of glass is said to represent the characteristics of the water element 'because it has no shape and every shape', and its situation is all the more auspicious because it stands right on the water's edge. As water is regarded by Feng Shui as the element of communication—and all the arts fall into this category—it is no wonder that the Opera House has earned such a worldwide reputation for generating outstanding music.

The story continued as I journeyed homewards across the Pacific. In the United States, which also has a high percentage of Chinese emigrants, I found evidence of Feng Shui being utilised in cities like Los Angeles, San Francisco and New York. Indeed, in San Francisco there were several professional Feng Shui *xiansheng* offering their services to the local emigrant population—and by all accounts also finding a demand from white Americans for household advice and consultations through the medium of the 'Eight Trigrams' about the future in matters of health, wealth and romance.

All along the West Coast there were stories of the spread of Feng Shui and, in the centre of Hollywood at Beverly Hills, one classic example of a building fulfilling its requirements in the most spectacular style. This is the glass 'palace' known as the I. M. Pei Building, which is the headquarters of the most powerful agent in the film business, Mike Ovitz. Carefully aligned to the local landscape and furnished to ensure balance and harmony, the building might be described as the most successful Feng Shui location in the world—certainly it is the centre of Ovitz's empire of megabucks and megastars. As if to underline the influence of the I. M. Pei building, an exclusive Rolls-Royce showroom stands immediately opposite.

New York also has a large Chinese population, but here the Feng Shui of its buildings has been created in what probably amounts to an unconscious search for the same elements which make it so valuable to people. The Rockefeller Centre in the middle of Manhattan, for example, has the kind of corridors which enable *Chi* to flow freely over the constant bustle of activity in the buildings, while the seasonal plants in the central open space help soften the harsh lines of the skyscrapers and bring the environment closer to nature. Without realising why, an American expert in Feng Shui told me, this is why so many New Yorkers gravitate there to find relaxation.

The Lincoln Centre, with its five sweeping, glass-filled arches, is also ideal for conducting beneficial influences into the building. Better still, the organ-like shape of the Guggenheim Museum, designed by the famous American architect, Frank Lloyd Wright, incorporates the best principles of Feng Shui by symbolising the continuity of nature and avoiding the sharp corners which attract bad *Sha*.

Back in the United Kingdom, I discovered that Feng Shui had also been subconsciously influencing the building of properties for centuries. Indeed, according to author Vincent Scully in his book *The Earth, The Temple and the Gods* (1976), 'A number of the megalithic monuments in Europe—Stonehenge in particular—have symbolic astronomical features and significant legends which suggest that their original function was in connection with Feng Shui practice in prehistoric antiquity.'

Another expert in this field, Nigel Pennick, also feels that some of the hills in the British Isles which are crowned with monuments and standing stones may have been utilised by earlier peoples for favourable alignments, in much the same manner as the Chinese used Feng Shui. Writing in his book *The Ancient Science of Geomancy* (1979), Pennick says:

The intrinsic geometry underlying all material things is the basis for geomantic architecture, which is required to harmonise with its purpose and position on the surface of the planet. Between geomantically determined sites, the alignments rediscovered by researchers like Black, Bennett, Watkins and Heinsch appear to have been known under different names to different cultures: the spirit paths of Chinese Feng Shui; the fairy roads of Ireland; the Royal Roads of England, etc. This geometry is, in short, the universal means by which the intrinsic oneness of the universe may be comprehended.

Although time has not allowed me to carry out further investigations into what other constructions there might be in Britain that owe something to the same principles as Feng Shui, it is worth mentioning the case of Sir William Chambers who redesigned Kew Gardens in 1757. He took for his example the spontaneous irregularity and asymmetrical planning that he had learned was the inspiration for many Chinese gardens, as he later described:

> Something of this I have seen in some places, but heard more of it from others, who have lived among the Chinese, a people whose way of thinking seems to lie as wide of ours in Europe as their country does. Their greatest reach of imagination is employed in contriving figures where the beauty shall be great and strike the eye, but without any order or disposition of parts, that shall be commonly or easily observed. And though we have hardly any notion of this sort of beauty, yet they have a particular word to express it, and where they find it hits their eye at first sight, they say the *Sharawadgi* is fine or is admirable, or any such expression of esteem.

The word *Sharawadgi* is almost certainly a corruption of Feng Shui as a Western ear might hear it spoken in Chinese, and this is surely what Sir William meant when describing his inspiration for Kew. Today the gardens still stand as a monument to his vision . . . and, perhaps, a tribute to the ancient Chinese art.

A similar comparison has also been spotlighted in the heart of London, on the famous shopping thoroughfare of Oxford

Street. It was first observed by a sharp-eyed lady traveller, Lady Susan Townley, not long after returning to England from a trip to China, during which she had evidently learned about the Feng Shui of buildings. Writing in *My Chinese Note Book*, published in 1904, she declared: 'The Chinese believe that the roofs of houses adjoining should never be built on the same level. Hence the Feng Shui of Oxford Street would be considered good while that of most Parisian thoroughfares bad.'

These, then, are just a few of the more visible sights of Feng Shui that can be seen at various places around the world. Its invisible influence, however, is everywhere, as I hope I have demonstrated in the pages of this book. I invite you to take advantage of its principles in your own life, for it is not lightly. that this very ancient and enduring art, distilled from centuries of Chinese knowledge, has also been called 'The Science of Happiness' . . .

BIBLIOGRAPHY

Listed here are the various works I consulted during the research for this book. They are all recommended to the reader keen to learn about the history and development of Feng Shui and the more complex details of its practice.

Baker, H. *Ancestral Images* (South China Morning Post Ltd, Hong Kong, 1979).

Ball, Dyer. *Things Chinese* (John Murray, London, 1892).

Bloomfield, F. *The Book of Chinese Beliefs* (Ballantine Books, New York, 1989).

Bloodworth, Dennis. *The Chinese Looking Glass* (Farrar Straus & Giroux, New York, 1980).

Burkhardt, V. R. *Chinese Creeds and Customs* (South China Morning Post Ltd, Hong Kong, 1982).

Cumming, Constance, *Wanderings in China* (William Blackwood, Edinburgh, 1896).

De Groot, J. J. M. *The Religious System of China* (Brill, Leiden, 1897).

Doré, Henry. *Researches into Chinese Superstitions* (Tusewei Press, Shanghai, 1929).

Edkins, J. *Feng Shui* (Chinese Recorder and Missionary Society, Foochow, 1872).

Eitel, E. J. *Feng Shui: The Science of the Sacred Landscape in Old China* (Trubner, London, 1873).

Feuchtwang, S. D. R. *An Anthropological Analysis of Chinese Geomancy* (Vithagna Press, Laos, 1974).

Henry, B. C. *The Cross and the Dragon* (Anson Randolph, New York, 1885).

Holcombe, Chester, *The Real Chinaman* (Hodder & Stoughton, London, 1895).

Hsu, Francis, *Under The Ancestors' Shadow* (Stanford University Press, 1971).

Johnston, R. F. *Lion and Dragon in Northern China* (John Murray, London, 1910).

Knapp, Ronald G. *The Chinese House* (Oxford University Press, 1990).

Lip, Evelyn. *Chinese Geomancy* (Times Books, Singapore, 1979).

O'Brian, Joanna, and Kwok Man Ho. *Elements of Feng Shui* (Element Books, England, 1991).

Pennick, Nigel. *The Ancient Science of Geomancy* (Thames & Hudson, London, 1979).

Pennick, Nigel. *Earth Harmony* (Century Hutchinson, London, 1987).

Porter, L. L. *Feng Shui: Or How The Chinese Keep in Tune with Nature* (Chinese Recorder and Missionary Society, Foochow, 1920).

Rossbach, S. *Feng Shui: The Chinese Art of Placement* (E. P. Dutton Inc, New York, 1984).

Skinner, Stephen. *The Living Earth Manual of Feng Shui* (Routledge & Kegan Paul, London, 1982).

Skinner, Stephen. *The Oracle of Geomancy* (Warner Books, New York, 1977).

Turner, F. S. *Feng Shui* (Cornhill Magazine Ltd., London, 1874).

Walters, Derek. *Feng Shui* (Pagoda Books, London, 1988).

Wheatley, Paul. *The Pivot of the Four Quarters* (Aldine Press, Chicago, 1971).

Wu, N. I. *Chinese Architecture* (Studio Vista, London, 1968).

INDEX